Fixer and Fighter

The boats of Newhaven and Folkestone and Dover,
To Dieppe and Boulogne and to Calais cross over;
And in each of these runs there is not a square yard
Where the English and French haven't fought and fought hard!
(The French Wars, Rudyard Kipling)

Fixer and Fighter

The Life of Hubert de Burgh, Earl of Kent, 1170–1243

Brian Harwood

Pen & Sword
MILITARY

First published in Great Britain in 2016 by
Pen & Sword Military
an imprint of
Pen & Sword Books Ltd
47 Church Street
Barnsley
South Yorkshire
S70 2AS

ISBN 978 1 47387 736 8

A CIP catalogue record for this book is available from the British
Library

Typeset in Ehrhardt by
Mac Style Ltd, Bridlington, East Yorkshire
Printed and bound in the UK by CPI Group (UK) Ltd,
Croydon, CRO 4YY

Pen & Sword Books Ltd incorporates the imprints of Pen & Sword
Archaeology, Atlas, Aviation, Battleground, Discovery, Family
History, History, Maritime, Military, Naval, Politics, Railways, Select,
Transport, True Crime, and Fiction, Frontline Books, Leo Cooper,
Praetorian Press, Seaforth Publishing and Wharncliffe.

For a complete list of Pen & Sword titles please contact
PEN & SWORD BOOKS LIMITED
47 Church Street, Barnsley, South Yorkshire, S70 2AS, England
E-mail: enquiries@pen-and-sword.co.uk
Website: www.pen-and-sword.co.uk

Contents

Dedicated to the memory of my late cousin – Geoffrey Clements ACII, FSA.

A Home Counties man born and bred, Geoffrey – man of many talents – from his eighteen-year tenure as treasurer to the *Victoria County History of Essex*, and later as its vice-president, knew well, and shared with me his encyclopaedic knowledge of the southern counties exploits of Hubert de Burgh, Earl of Kent.

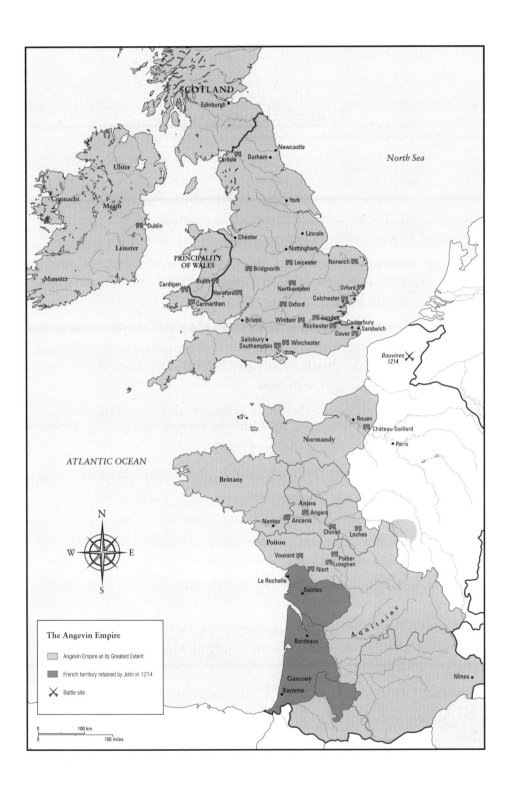

The Angevin Empire

Angevin Empire at its Greatest Extent

French territory retained by John in 1214

Battle site

List of Illustrations

Dover Castle. For his implacable, undefeated defence of this 'key to the kingdom', Hubert de Burgh was made Earl of Kent. (*BLOM*)

The four momentous Plantagenet kings, with 'The Young Henry' in the centre. Henry II (top left), Richard I (top right), John (bottom left) and Henry III. (*British Library, MS Roy.14 C VII f.9*)

Hubert de Burgh's men-at-arms despatching the piratical French Admiral, Eustace the Monk, on the gunwales of Eustace's own *Great Ship of Bayonne* during the Battle of Sandwich, 24 August 1217. (*Matthew Paris MS 16. Folio 52, Corpus Christi College, Cambridge*)

The head of pirate Eustace the Monk being paraded through Canterbury after the defeat of the French fleet off Sandwich by Hubert de Burgh, 24 August 1217. (*Mary Evans Picture Library*)

A crossbowman arming his weapon. (*British Library, Addn MS 42130, f.56*)

'A mail-clad Plantagenet knight draws his sword.' (*Lutterworth Press*, A Knight and his Armour, *1961*)

Prince Louis of France and his generals arriving to invade England. (*Corpus Christi, Cambridge, MS 016 f.46v*)

Cogs in Battle. Their distinctive fore and aft castles clearly seen. (*British Library*)

Château Gaillard. Richard the Lionheart's 'Saucy Castle' on the Seine at Les Andelys. It fell with little resistance to King Philip of France in 1203. (*France Tourisme*)

Rochester Castle. After Hubert de Burgh undermined the keep in November 1215, the present Poitevin cylindrical tower replaced it. (*English Heritage*)

John 'Softsword' with his dogs. When not terrorising his subjects, John was following the hounds in one of his many royal forests. There still remain various 'King John's Hunting Lodge' buildings in today's residual forested areas. (*British Library, MS Roy 20 A II*)

King John considering his fate after sealing Magna Charta at Runnymede on 10 June 1215. (*M. Dovaston*, Story of the British Nation Vol.1, *385, Hutchinson 1922*)

Falaise Castle. At Falaise in April 1203 King John murdered Prince Arthur of Brittany, the rightful heir to the English throne. (*Marianne Majerus*)

The murder of Prince Arthur of Brittany, heir to the English throne, in April 1203, as imagined by William Shakespeare in his *The Tragedie of King John*. Here Hubert is portrayed by the great John Kemble in the 1790s. (*J.Rogers/W.Hamilton (Mary Evans)*)

Chinon Castle. Hubert defended this massive fortress against a French army for eighteen months until June 1205. (*France Tourisme*)

Donjon de Niort. Hubert's operational headquarters when Seneschal of Poitou, 1213–15. It was never besieged. (*France Tourisme*)

The Battle of Bouvines Bridge. The victory here of the French over the combined British force on 27 July 1214 marked the beginning of the end for English continental ambitions. (*Bibliothèque Nationale, Ms Français 2609, f.219v*)

Plan of the Anglo Angevin continental provinces. After the Battle of Bouvines this Angevin empire quickly disintegrated. (The Struggle for Mastery: Britain 1066–1284, *p.xii, D. Carpenter, Allen Lane, 2003*)

Old St Paul's (1085–1666) much as Hubert saw it. It dominated London's skyline as does the Shard today. (*The Builder Ltd.,1962*)

Whitehall Palace c1570 by Ralph Agas. It grew from Hubert de Burgh's Thames-side mansion and would eventually cover 23 acres. (*Museum of London*)

Hadleigh Castle in Essex. Built in the 1220s by Hubert de Burgh as his early warning fortification against Thames estuary incursions into his homeland. (*English Heritage*)

Creake Abbey. Founded in 1206 by Sir Robert and Lady Alice of Nerford, Hubert's East Anglian neighbours. It was granted Abbey status in October 1231 through Hubert's influence. Sir Robert was Hubert's deputy fleet commander at the Battle of Sandwich. (*English Heritage*)

Hubert de Burgh depicted in sanctuary at Merton Priory where Hubert stayed in hiding from King John's 'hit squad' during July 1232. (*British Library, Matthew Paris Historia Anglorum, Roy.14.C.VII. fol.119v*)

The original Norman gateway of Merton Priory. Hubert de Burgh would have passed through it many times. (*Merton Council*)

Self-portrait of Matthew Paris, St Alban's monk and Hubert's oldest friend and confidant. (*British Library*)

Magna Charta. The best preserved of the four surviving copies of the document. (*British Library Cot. MS Augustus II 106*)

Skenfrith Castle in Monmouthshire, the most used of Hubert de Burgh's 'Three Castles of the Justiciar'. The other two were nearby Grosmont and White Castle. (*CADW: Welsh Historic Monuments*)

Skenfrith Castle. A reconstruction of how it looked in Hubert's time. (*CADW: Chris Jones-Jenkins*)

The Seal of Winchelsea. The ship – an improved version of the Cog – is weighing anchor and setting sail, with trumpeters sounding the departure. (*National Maritime Museum, Greenwich*)

Second coronation of Henry III, taking place at Westminster Abbey on 17 May 1220. Henry is still the only English monarch to have two coronations. (*Cambridge, Corpus Christi College 16, fol.56*)

A thirteenth-century Gascony wine jug – a drinking vessel very familiar to Hubert de Burgh. (*Carisbrooke Castle Museum, I.O.W./English Heritage*)

St Bartholomew's Chapel, Sandwich, Kent. Built in 1217 by the Sandwich parishioners with the treasure taken from the French fleet defeated by Hubert de Burgh on 24 August – St Bartholomew's Day. (*1917 Postcard*)

The late twelfth-century murals at the Chapelle Sainte-Radegonde at Chinon Castle. Henry II and Queen Eleanour are depicted, but other family identities are open to question.

Preface

Fixer and Fighter is the story of Hubert de Burgh, Earl of Kent. He was a fighting man, used to wiping from his armour the blood and entrails of his enemies. A man who saved the throne of his 9-year-old King during a successful French invasion of England. A man who sent that same French army packing, permanently, sinking their fleet. A man who countersigned Magna Charta, and then supervised its update to the betterment of the English nation. A man who protected and modernized the English economy, even to counting the pennies. A man who fought the English cause across the continent, often hand-to-hand. A man who frightened the Vatican. A man who perfected the art of castle warfare. A man as lethal and uncompromising in the political arena as in the battlefield.

A man who held Dover Castle against all the odds and saved the nation. A man who laid the foundations for an English national government. A man of paramount ambition and equivalent achievement. An ultimate survivor who outlived all his enemies to die peacefully in his own bed.

But, in contrast, William Shakespeare could be said to have initiated the bad press that Hubert de Burgh has had to suffer for centuries since. With the erroneous slur on his reputation in his *The Life and Death of King John*, the playwright makes Hubert the villain of the piece as being instrumental in the murder (in 1204) of Prince Arthur of Brittany, rightful heir to the English throne. In fact Hubert protected Arthur with his life until King John had other ideas. But the die was cast and the calumny continued to accrete, as in Charles Dickens' highly imaginative *History of England*. Later historians have done little to break this 'anti-Hubert' mould. Rather than seeking to question whether a statesman of such towering personality was really such damaged goods, those writers continue to perpetuate the calumny; their conclusions, though, appearing only in piecemeal studies of confined aspects of Hubert de Burgh's life – a popular biography of all of that life appears never to have been written. In *Fixer and Fighter* I set out refreshed thinking about Hubert's contribution to the nation. As each chapter progresses, the reader will start to breathe the atmosphere of anti-Angevin antipathy that progressively pervaded the country in those times. The reader will then see how this antipathy crystallized into a life or death face-off between the two main protagonists of this story – Hubert de Burgh, the dyed-in-the-wool Englishman, and Peter des Roches, the haughty and ruthless immigrant Angevin bishop of Winchester. Both seeking to be the dominant political influence in the country – only one could win! The point I try to make overall in this account (and one missed by other analysts) is that, for all his shortcomings, Hubert de Burgh was the right man in the right place at the right time for England, in its hour of most need – and on more than one occasion. What emerges is a persuasive parallel between Hubert de Burgh and Winston Churchill.

This narrative describes life in Magna Charta England as seen through the eyes of a senior courtier who lived through and experienced it all in those decades of perennial social unrest as an Angevin administration tried, by invasion and aggressive political duplicity, to make England a French colony. The role of the Vatican in supporting the Angevin cause in England is highlighted, as is the native English resistance to that role, largely initiated by Hubert de Burgh's influence. This influence is seen additionally creating a first ever platform for truly English government as, on many occasions, Hubert de Burgh led from the front, including for years ruling England for the boy king, Henry III. From the first page I try to put the reader just behind the shoulder of Hubert as he progressively climbs the often near fatal slippery pole of medieval court life. How he achieves it – and lives (only just!) to tell us the tale in the records of his time – is as gripping a narrative as it is sometimes almost unbelievable, but it all really happened: including the only other successful invasion of England since 1066. And I take pains to remind readers how unique is the legacy of this great Englishman's contribution to his nation's well-being. Sir Winston concurs as, in his book *The Island Race* (p. 52), he states – 'Hubert throughout his tenure stood for the policy of doing the least possible to recover the King's French domains. He resisted the Papacy in its efforts to draw money at all costs out of England for its large European schemes. He maintained order, and as the King grew up he restrained the Court party which was forming about him from making inroads upon the Charter. His was entirely the English point of view.'

To my knowledge Hubert de Burgh has never been the subject of any detailed biographical treatment since the 1952 print of C Ellis' *A Study in Constancy*. However, Ellis' complex tome appears principally focused on the background political aspects of Hubert de Burgh's time rather than the man. The few other studies I was able to find appear in esoteric journals and deal – mostly briefly – with highly selective aspects of his time and life: I found no authority with an overall coverage of the man specifically. Nor, throughout my extensive researches on him did I find any other 'popular' biography in existence. No one today (including myself) can look back to a period eight centuries distant and with certainty set out what happened then, which is why, in contrast, the present work intends just to introduce Hubert de Burgh to a new public. It does not set out to discuss in detail long held, and often widely varying, viewpoints concerning the vindictive political times in which he lived.

Refreshingly, one authority (originally published in 1905, reprinted in 2005) does provide a rare laudatory profile, albeit just a very brief chapter, of Hubert. The school-book study by HE Marshall (*Our Island Story*, Galore Park/Civitas, 2005) represents a first attempt in modern times to recognize this forgotten Norfolk statesman of clearly intimidating presence and charisma. Contemporary authorities describing (usually sketchily) Hubert's actions in those violent medieval times run the gamut of opinions. They tend to either attribute to him the role of shining national hero, or grudgingly admit that he may have made a 'bit-part' appearance in some of the events described; while others (particularly Channel Islands sources) even question whether he was ever significantly involved at all. Given these polarities of opinion, in this account I have endeavoured to find a way which summarizes Hubert's background, life and times with the best equality I can manage: progressing through the least contentious middle dry ground, avoiding the swamps of extreme viewpoints bordering its either side. My best hope is that an invigorated debate about the life of this forgotten hero results.

Much that we know about Hubert de Burgh, his life and his times, comes from the pen of Matthew Paris, or Parisiensis, as he signed himself. Matthew Paris was a monk of St Alban's Abbey, Hertfordshire, who first took Holy Orders there on 1 January 1217, (St Agnes' Day). His date of birth is estimated as *c.*1200. He would live until 1259. His inborn gifts with words and pictures immediately marked him out for a role in the Abbey scriptorium working under the guidance of that other great St Alban's chronicler, Roger of Wendover. Their joint endeavours to record and depict the lives, personalities and events of their times progressed together until Roger's death in 1236.

Although theoretically monastically secluded, Paris took every opportunity to keep himself in touch with the outside world and its happenings. He was also allowed access to the huge mass of royal and governmental documentation that the Abbey received, year in year out. In today's terminology he could be seen as an 'information geek'. He stored news items for future reference, particularly those which were of anti-Angevin content or purpose. Hence he soon became aware of Hubert de Burgh's actions and policies of similar vein. Alongside his rabid interest in all things anti-French, Paris slowly accumulated the material for his magnum opus, his *Chronica Majora* – his history of England from the Creation to his contemporary times. Written in Latin, it continued on from a basis set out by Roger of Wendover, and it remains one of our most informative and powerful accounts of medieval life and times prevailing during Hubert de Burgh's lifetime. For instance, the renewed Forest Charter of 1225 Paris sets out in his *Chronica excerpta* (extracts) in a more readable form than the original. As the Oxford DNB states, 'Foreigners riled him. The Savoyards and the Poitevins, he felt, greedily fattened themselves on English revenues and deprived native Englishmen of wealth and rank. The French as a whole he denounced as proud and effeminate.' Paris supported all of Hubert de Burgh's efforts to evict them from English government. After Hubert's success at the Battle of Sandwich, Paris eulogizes him saying: 'When Hubert, after his miraculous victory, reached the English coast, all the bishops who were in that quarter came out to meet him, clad in their sacred robes … singing psalms and praising God.' While Roger of Wendover's account seems to imply that Hubert took more of a back seat in the action, Paris had no doubts where the initiative for the sea victory lay, and unambiguously said so in his chronicle. He also recorded sequences of the battle in pictures, coloured in vermilion and green tints to highlight the action. As the reader will see when, in 1222,

Hubert had to 'discipline' an 'irrational mob' of Londoners, both Paris and Wendover pulled no punches in detailing the measures taken by Hubert to restore civil order. Consequently in this narrative the reader will find Matthew Paris interjecting more and more into the events of Hubert's time being described. Should any reader so wish to study the original Matthew Paris documentation, then much of his work, literary and pictorial, is held at Corpus Christi College, Cambridge, while a further collection is held at the British Library.

My Select Bibliography lists some of the many and varied, old and new, avenues I have travelled down in this attempt to define Hubert de Burgh for a modern generation; however, additional to these authorities must be my grateful recognition of the many record offices, universities, libraries and the like who have made selfless efforts in making available their resources to me. I remain indebted to them for their informed and kind advice in assisting my quest for factual help. I cannot list them all here, but principal amongst these are Norfolk Studies Library, Norwich; Dover Castle; Dover Museum; Dover Reference Library; Hadleigh Castle Country Park; Surrey History Centre, Woking; St Bartholomew's Hospital, Sandwich; Rochester Castle; the Dean and Chapter, Rochester Cathedral; the Dean and Chapter, Salisbury Cathedral; the City of London Guildhall Library; Southwark Local Studies Library; The British Library; National Gallery; Royal Shakespeare Company; Lambeth Reference Library, Jersey Library, Priaulx Library, Guernsey, and the Bibliothèque nationale de France. Lastly, but not in any way least, I must thank my Commissioning Editor at Pen & Sword, Philip Sidnell, for his inexhaustible patience in coping with the demands of the author – a long paid up member of the very elderly brigade. I must too acknowledge the generous help given by my son James and daughter-in-law Su who, combining their skills helped smooth the passage of the documentation and the production of the illustrations. Nor must I forget the efforts 'beyond the call of duty' expended by the expert Wadhurst Library staff in the trials that I continually placed before them with my requests for the most obscure titles – they never failed.

Chapter 1

Richard I 'the Lionheart' 1189–1199

East Anglia to Westminster: the young Hubert comes to Court

The year is 1185. A sturdy, determined teenager emerges through the front door of an inn near Aldgate, just east of London's city walls. Hubert de Burgh, blinking in the bright spring sunrise, has just recovered from a miry trek of nearly a week from the family home, Burgh-next-Aylsham, near Norwich, down to London. For his safety he had travelled in a party with a dozen other merchants and clerks: they had earlier gone their separate ways. Hubert's elder brother William, a prominent civil servant with Richard the Lionheart, had pulled strings for him to be accepted into a junior post at the dynamic, animated Angevin court now settling into a permanent site by the Thames at Westminster. Hubert, away from home for the first time, has detailed route instructions given him by William to get from the inn to Westminster. We also can take the opportunity to familiarize ourselves with London as it was in Hubert's day, and follow in his footsteps as he sets off to find London's main dock at Queenhithe, and a boat to Westminster.

Following his instructions, Hubert walks to the old Aldgate passage through the London Roman wall remnants. Passing through that gate he sees the huge Holy Trinity Priory complex in front of him so, to get down towards the river, he takes a left turn around the Priory. But as he does this, for just a second or two, he glances back at the Priory then, in a kind of déjà vu twinge, crosses himself, before heading off to his next landmark. Rounding a bend Hubert's next landmark blots out everything nearby – the Tower of London! Its implacable 90ft high walls, completed by 1100, are topped by sentry walks, with ground floor entrances protected by surly and burly glowering guards. To stop and stare is not an option: Hubert hurries on past this beating heart of London commerce and discipline, remembering to keep the river to his left. After five minutes the alleys become side streets and he finds himself looking along half a mile of market stalls: it is 'The Longe Shoppe' – today Cheapside. Nearby are poultry stalls, further on he could see woollen cloth (drapery) on sale by a linen stall (mercery). Every possible saleable commodity is being hawked in a deafening commotion of traders' shouts: at this time Cheapside was the busiest shopping market in Britain. Hubert had heard on his journey that a 100 sq ft stall here could command an annual rent of £1.50: a sum that would get 20 acres of good land in East Anglia. As he takes his breather Hubert is dumbstruck by the colossal cathedral of St Paul towering over the far end of the 'Shoppe'. Towering literally – its soon to be completed spire surging a huge 520ft upwards – the highest in northern Europe! It was as compelling a London sight then as The Shard is today. The cathedral of St Paul is, in fact, the east minster; the west minster, where Hubert is headed, is dedicated to St Peter.

Taking the next alley sloping down to the Thames Hubert starts pushing his way through the clamouring throng of dockside workers. Everyone has something to do – to push, pull or carry, and everything is heavy, and Hubert is in the way of it all, his senses assailed by an all-pervading atmosphere of spices, Stockholm tar, sewage, and a veritable babel of dialects. One ship he notices flying the Templars' Red Cross emblem. He thought he recalled that Dunwich port, near his home, on the Norfolk/Suffolk border was known for its long-standing links with the Gascony wine trade via the Templars: that Order had a small estate with chapel at Dunwich from which it managed its East Anglian/continental trade. (What Hubert didn't know was that this legendary entrepreneurial Order also ran a highly profitable cross-river trading business from their Southwark market centre called Withyflete – today Borough Market.) After several further minutes of dodging dockers and horses Hubert gets to the Queenhithe passenger pier. Clambering down into the Thames tilt boat he finds a seat and watches the Port of London activity as the boatman waits for the tide to turn.

Queenhithe Dock (it's still there today, just off Upper Thames Street) would be closely associated with Hubert in future times, so a thumbnail sketch of its origins will be useful here. Following his ousting of the Vikings, Alfred and his son-in-law Ethelred set to providing London ('Lundenwic') with a state of the art shipping terminal between 886 and 899. It wasn't too difficult as the Romans had already left their stone paved dock storage area on the north bank of the Thames, just a couple of hundred yards upstream from today's Southwark Bridge. It was an inspired investment for the Alfred/Ethelred partnership in that the creation of this riverside trading estate fixed permanently the role of London as the commercial capital of the newly united kingdom. By the time of Henry I (1100–1135) it was a booming business centre specializing in imports of grain and wine – but Henry's wife, Matilda, wanted some of the income for her philanthropic 'good works'. To keep the peace Henry made over to her most of the dock income giving the dock its 'Queenhithe' identity it still retains today. The royal consorts were subsequently granted, *ex officio*, the port income successively down to 1247 when the City financier Richard of Cornwall transferred the grant in perpetuity to the City of London. Hubert would in later times (1225) witness the monarch, Henry III, commanding the Constable of the Tower of London to arrest ships of the Cinque Ports found working on the Thames and compel them to bring their cargoes to Queenhithe only. Queenhithe dock, founded 886, still survives today in a modest mercantile role.

With the tide turning, Hubert's ferry cast off for Westminster. Looking back from midstream as the river curved to the west, Hubert could see the new Thames Bridge being built out from the north bank on stone-filled piers. It was started in 1176: Hubert would see its eventual 1000ft-long, 20-arch completion some thirty years later. Along the riverbanks he sees dotted landing stages of private mansions: a kind of marine millionaires' row. They house the magnates and movers settling in at the new Westminster-located seat of government. As the tilt-boat swung in towards its destination Hubert recalled his brother's warning against trying to get to Westminster on foot. It was nearly three miles from Aldgate, clogged with traffic at all hours, and that he might miss the vital left fork for Westminster at the village of Charing. If he carried straight on there, Hubert would have ended up in the fetid, desolate and deserted St James' marshlands where only a leper hospital eked out its isolated existence, a few of its inmates leprous Crusaders. As Hubert lands at Westminster stairs we leave him to find his way into his new world; to meet and mingle with these magnates and movers who between them administered an Angevin kingdom stretching from the Pyrenees north to Hadrian's Wall: meanwhile we take a quick look at his background and, as well, set out his qualifications for the job.

His parents were related to Alice and Robert de Nereford of Norfolk. However, Hubert's descendancy from the de Burghs is overcrowded with possible claimants – no clear paternal line can at present be established beyond reasonable doubt. Nor can the relationship with the East Anglian place-name 'Burgh' be followed with any certainty, there being a multitude of Burghs across those eastern counties, but the best informed sources place Hubert's Burgh as being Burgh-next-Aylsham in the Hundred of South Erpingham. What is certain is that Hubert had three brothers; William, Geoffrey and Thomas – though again parentage of each of the three is not traceable without doubt. William had already started to carve out a career of great achievement in Ireland; Geoffrey stayed in East Anglia to eventually hold high office within the Church, while Thomas followed a life of lesser attainment than his brothers in living as a lord of the manor in Norfolk. Each of the brothers would, in due course, have reason to be grateful for Hubert's influence upon their lives.

Hubert himself was now taking his first steps towards aggregating that influence. It was the 15-year-old's first journey outside his home county. Until now his world had mostly been limited to educational periods spent at the famous East Anglian teaching centres such as Ely, under the great bishop, Geoffrey Ridel, and Bury St Edmunds under Abbot Samson, who founded at Bury a free school for poor scholars. It is interesting that Bishop Ridel was also a senior courtier to Henry II and, as well, an Exchequer Baron. Might some conversational snippets during tutorials have sparked Hubert's interest? He would himself one day become an Exchequer Baron. At these centres of learning Hubert's achievements, particularly his writing and linguistic skills, had so impressed his tutors that his elder brother William found him an opening at the Treasury. Left at home to continue their education were his younger brothers Thomas and Geoffrey; as noted both would later benefit from Hubert's success which was about to start in the court of John, Count of Mortain.[1] A further sponsorship to Hubert was possibly the great East Anglian neighbouring family of the Warennes. Later, in c.1200, at his home in Castle Acre, Norfolk, Earl Hamelin of Warenne signed himself as a witness on probably the first charter document assigned to the young civil servant Hubert for him to process.

At this period educational opportunities available to those with natural literacy gifts were opening up across Europe under the influence of imported Arabic, Byzantine and eastern learning. The best teachers at work in Britain gained their scholarship knowledge from studies at continental cities from which would emerge the first universities: Paris 1160, Naples 1224, Padua 1222, Salamanca 1134, Bologna 1088, for example. Hubert would have honed his educational skills on a subject base of Latin grammar, logic and rhetoric, arithmetic, astronomy, geometry and perhaps some musical studies. A man achieving well in these disciplines could expect to pursue a fast-track career in government or ecclesiastical administration. And, as one modern authority states, '… by 1200 the English monarchy was far in advance of the French in its employment of "schoolmen".'[2]

When Hubert came to London, his brother William had already been an influential courtier for some years engaged in securing the crown estates in Ireland, and was on the staff of Henry II's youngest son, Prince John, Count of Mortain. As with the rest of the royal Court, John had close links with the Treasury, a department run by another top civil servant also from East Anglia, Richard FitzNigel of Ely. Holding the post of Court Treasurer, he had offices in Westminster along King Street, the main approach road to the palace of Westminster, today Whitehall. Hubert would be in contact with – and almost certainly employed in – Richard's department, and must have lodged in rooms nearby. In fact in later times Hubert's career clearly demonstrates an intimate knowledge of the Treasurer's office which he could only have acquired at first hand. Always a pious man – and East Anglians were proud and dedicated churchgoers – Hubert, from an early age, could recite the full Latin Mass off by heart. He would have taken the interest to walk along, psalter in hand, to have a look at the vast new Benedictine St Peter's Abbey, consecrated by King Edward the Confessor on 28 December 1065, just across the road from the royal palace and the governing force in the lay community of Westminster. How Westminster then looked as Hubert strolled around it, was described in his journal by Thomas à Becket's secretary, William Fiztstephen,

Westminster rises on the river bank the King's Hall being of the greatest splendour with outworks and bastions … outside their houses are the

citizens' gardens, side by side yet spacious and splendid, and set about
with trees. To the north lie arable fields, pasture land and lush, level
meadows with brooks flowing everywhere within them, which do turn
the wheels of water mills ... Close by is the opening of a mighty forest,
with timbered copses and the lairs of wild beasts, stags and does, wild
boars and bulls.

Fitzstephen viewed the inhabitants as 'everywhere respected above all
others for their civil demeanour, their good apparel, their table and their
discourse'. On the other hand Richard of Devizes, a Winchester monk, in
his travelogue of English townships written about the same time, found
nothing to exalt: 'All sorts of men crowd together [in London] from every
country under the heavens, and each brings his own vices and customs.
No one lives there without falling into crime ... the number of braggarts
and parasites is infinite. Actors and jesters, smooth-skinned lads, Moors,
flatterers, effeminates, pederasts, belly-dancers, sorceresses, extortioners,
night-wanderers, magicians, mimes, beggars, buffoons, all this tribe fill the
houses. If you do not wish to live with evil-doers, do not live in London.'

On his journey south Hubert had seen the great new castles erected at
Colchester and Norwich, similar to the London Tower: he recalled his
grandparents saying that 113 houses had been demolished to make room
for the Norwich one. This exemplified the theme of the invaders from a
century ago, monumental fortresses controlling their localities now dotted
across the countryside like colossal chessmen. Originally about one to each
of the new scheme of counties designed to change old shires into new
local administrative areas but now, by Hubert's time, the castle tally had
increased to some 500 across the whole country. Castles were either royal
and owned by the King (some forty-nine in 1154, to rise to at least ninety-
three in 1214), or were the private family property.[3] No new castle could
be built by a family without the King's prior permission, and all castles,
royal and family, had to be opened to random inspection by the King or
his nominated representatives on demand. Failure to do so represented a
treasonable act with the castellan likely to be sentenced to death. Every castle
housed its castellan (nominated by the King where royal), usually a knight,
often a courtier, who was retained by the King to impose the law of the

land through the castellan's subordinate county sheriffs. Around the castle the local villagers paid their due called 'ferm' (today 'farm') to work the castle's lands and, when required, to take up arms for a contractual forty-day period for any cause nominated by their castellan: though this latter military service obligation could often be commuted with an appropriate payment – a 'knight's fee'. To an exceptionally intelligent youth as Hubert it was clear that to be a castellan was to be a powerful man, and if a multiple castellan, even more so. Hubert set himself this target, and his uncompromising ambition to this end would see him refine his subsequent property acquisitions into almost an art form.

During his time at home Hubert had been on outings to the busy commercial ports of Yarmouth and Lowestoft and been fascinated by their bustling harbours, with vessels departing for and arriving from ports all along the eastern European seaboard from Scandinavia down to the Low Countries. He would have seen the quays stacked with timber oak from Germany, 'firre' from Norway, broad oak from the Baltic, stone from Boulogne and its nearby Herquelingues quarries, all to fulfil the seemingly endless Norman building programme of castles, monasteries and cathedrals across the country. As he watched the Thames shipping endlessly criss-crossing the river outside his window, the same innate marine instinct that took him on those outings confirmed to him now that he had made the right decision to forge a career for himself at this cross-channel commuting Court.

From his first days at Westminster Hubert would have made the acquaintance of the many mariners constantly plying to and fro between the English shore and the continental ports of the Angevin Empire; in so doing he progressively accumulated a sound first-hand education in shipping economics and logistics from their conversations. He would have learned too of the hazards encountered from pirates and other shipping of belligerent intent: such information he stored away for future reference in his filing cabinet mind. In these times the port of London was in competition with Bristol for continental trade, the latter being a principal importer from the Angevin lands through Bordeaux and Bayonne in Gascony of woad, needed as a blue dye for the burgeoning Bristol wool trade. Perhaps it could be thought that, in today's terms, Hubert's court career took off with 'a job in shipping', utilizing his combined skills in literacy, numeracy, and finance at the Westminster Treasury.

The Treasury itself had gradually migrated up to Westminster from the Saxon capital at Winchester over the past couple of decades and by the 1180s it had become an independent government office, its original London offices being sited between the present Whitehall Banqueting House and the Thames. The easy movement of monies to and from the provinces across the Channel was of prime importance to the Angevin administration, whose European Treasury was housed in the massive Chinon fortress in the Loire valley. Self-evidently, the port of London presented a far better point of treasure transit than the old capital landlocked in the Wessex plains. The assumption that Hubert's court induction was via the Treasury is fortified by the documented fact that, in later years, he would return there and purchase for himself the Treasurer's Westminster mansion, and in so doing demonstrated a clear prior knowledge of the property.

In his daily Court errands and gradually increasing responsibilities, Hubert worked, walked, talked and socialized with a wide range of influential Treasury and Court staff, a principal mentor being maybe Alexander Swereford, the chief writing clerk to the Treasurer, William of Ely. From about 1180, under Swereford's supervision, worked a team of writers (*scriptors*) who compiled the new seminal series of fiscal records of national income and expenditure called the Feet of Fines. These unique documents survive today as one of the great landmarks of Angevin organization, and from them we can identify those who signed their entries. Those Hubert could have known and worked alongside include writers like John of Stortford, Thomas of Newgate, Gervase the scribe, Louis of Rockingham, William de Castello, and Thomas of Chenille. These men were highly skilled drafters of documents and, in most cases, attorneys; many came not from Britain but from the Angevin empire abroad. Also based at the Treasury were the highly influential Maudit family; hereditary chamberlains appointed to organize the movement of treasure (coin and bullion) between Britain and the continent. They operated under the supervision of Walter of Coutances who had overall responsibility for treasure management. Other officials 'hands on' to the Court's cash included Sergeants of the Treasure, Waleran of Cricklade and John of Wyke.

To co-ordinate and clarify the efforts of this polyglot mix of differing skills – tellers, melters, writers, weighers, chamberlain's clerks, and so on – the previous Treasurer, Richard FitzNigel, had written a handbook at Henry II's request called '*A Dialogue of Treasury Practice*', which Hubert would certainly have had knowledge of, and probably read to broaden his administrative skills.[4] FitzNigel though, was keen to assert his guiding principle being that 'the science of the Exchequer consists in correct decisions rather than correct accounts'. In his contact with Swereford's department Hubert could have seen the surviving questionnaires from the Domesday compilation also transferred up from Winchester for safekeeping at the Treasury after the death of the Conqueror in 1087. Hubert, to his great interest, would have seen that these unique documents related to East Anglia and included his home borough (again he recalled his grandparents' acid comments on the original assessors' visits to his locality). As Swereford would have explained, these few remaining questionnaire surveys ('*inquisitiones*') had yet to be incorporated into Great Domesday but awaited the King's initiative on the matter; meanwhile they must be kept in safe custody.[5] (They were never to be incorporated.) Alexander Swereford was to leave his own 'user manual' to posterity, known as '*The Red Book of the Exchequer*'.

In so far as 'Court' as opposed to 'Treasury' staff was concerned, Hubert was at this time still very much on the outside looking in. Most of the men that he now met in passing for the first time had been appointed after John's elevation to Lord of Ireland in 1177 by Henry II, when John was only 10-years-old – John visited Ireland for just six months in 1185. Running his household subsequently were William de Cahaines as seneschal, assisted by Theobald Walter as butler. Holding the office of chamberlain (a post later filled by Hubert) was Alard Fitzwilliam; in joint authority with him was Roger de Planes who held another post Hubert would later aspire to, that of Justiciar. Various stewards and clerks peopled the lower ranks of John's Court such as, for example, Peter de Littlebury, Thomas de Husseburne, Adam de St Edmunds, and Ralph de Chichester. Other frequent attendees and hangers-on included Hamo de Valignes, Richard de Rivers, Walter de Dunstanville, William de la Falaise, Robert de Bretoil, Hugh de Malauney and Robert de la Mara. Of course each of these favoured individuals – they held great influence and property on both sides of the Channel – had their own agenda to try and rise and rise in John's circle. Few survived long to do so, but Hubert was to.

Because its kings spent much of their time on the continent, Hubert would have had to master the political geography of the Angevin kingdom ruled from Westminster. It stretched north from the Pyrenees to Scotland, and comprised a slippery kaleidoscope of principalities, dukedoms, and baronies whose ruling families changed their allegiances almost at every turn of the weather. Only *ad hoc* tentative truces and agreements of homage formed at each fickle change of political taste kept some semblance of peace. Also there continually interweaved a clandestine undercurrent of opportunist outlawry between all these social strata which periodically destabilized any agreement between the rulers and the ruled.[6] In these Angevin times it was impossible to draw a line between Englishmen and 'foreigners'. English kings and nobles ruled parts of France, and many people had commercial interests in both countries. To Hubert's credit he appears to have absorbed the political complexity of this Angevin knowledge base effortlessly: and he had to, for infinitely sterner tests of both his knowledge and character were just around the corner, also, as will be seen, he did not give a high priority to being popular in his management of any nobility's polarized interests.

Chapter 2

1189–1199 Castles and Crusades

These kings from Anjou – Henry II, Richard, John and Henry III – were characterized by their single-minded pursuit of their ambitions; ruthless, quick thinking, very short-fused, always looking to achieve their ends on a larger than life scale, and with little regard to the cost or consequences of their actions. Each in his own way was a significant analytical thinker – but they tended to focus more on their personal aims than on the national endeavour. The continental area they ruled comprised Brittany, Normandy, Maine, Anjou, Touraine, and the vast duchy of Aquitaine which then covered what is today virtually a quarter of south France; it had been acquired by Henry II's marriage to Eleanor of Aquitaine. Control of these English continental frontiers with France was effected through a line of castles erected at salient points from Rouen, the capital of Normandy, down to Poitiers, then south to Nimes.[1] As mentioned earlier, at one of the most formidable, Chinon, the Angevin Treasury was housed; from here all Angevin continental possessions and activities were financed.

Henry II spent much of his time on the continent solely to ensure the safety of his inherited dominions from the invasion threats of Philip, King of France, and likewise the plotting of his imprisoned wife, Eleanor of Aquitaine, with his sons Richard and John over their inheritance. Later, when his son Richard did eventually succeed to the throne, he too in his ten-year rule was to spend barely six months in England. During his brief English residency Richard only looked to the revenues of the kingdom to finance his obsession with Crusading – freeing Jerusalem from the Saracen invaders.

Hubert de Burgh was born into and lived his whole life through the Crusades era; the international economics and politics of Crusades' ethics and idealism coloured all his life's environment, both outside of and within the court. The Crusades were a persistent undercurrent of thought, surfacing and resurfacing randomly as undercurrents do, to intrude in the life at all levels of the people of those times in a way difficult to comprehend today. Instead, the modern concept of a 'Crusade' is that many 'good' militant European citizens formed themselves into armies and went off to Middle Eastern countries to fight against their 'bad' citizens, collectively defined as 'infidels', the ultimate aim being to create a Christian, as opposed to any other, religious discipline in the Holy Lands. Not an accurate assumption and virtually all Crusades eventually failed in their ultimate aim, the permanent imposition of Roman Christianity upon a reluctant recipient. All Crusades were backed, if not financed by, the Vatican, with the aim of removing any dissident threat to the universally powerful papal authority of the day. Consequently any belligerent initiative taken by a local monarch or prince aimed at subduing an element of recalcitrant populace, if it was deemed by the Vatican to be in their interests, was defined as a 'Crusade'.[2] During Hubert de Burgh's lifetime, there were some twenty-five papally approved 'Crusade' conflicts, many being fought concurrently, creating religious upheaval in Spain, Flanders, Portugal, Cyprus, Livonia (today Latvia), Denmark, Constantinople, southern France, Transylvania, Estonia, Bosnia, Prussia, Mallorca, and Germany. And this isn't taking into account the major Holy Land conflicts, namely, the Second Crusade – 1147–9, Third Crusade – 1189–92, the Fourth Crusade – 1198–1204, and the Fifth Crusade – 1217–29. (The 'First Crusade' was initiated by Pope Urban II in 1095.)

Kings and military leaders with plenty of money went on Crusades; their subordinate armies went along for the adventure and the takings – under a (threadbare) cloak of religious sincerity. Mostly these forces comprised polyglot collections of mercenary ruffians, often including individuals from the country being subdued. So far as the sponsorship went, the Vatican looked kindly on the tax affairs of those who had registered a vow with the Roman authorities to go on Crusade. Even if they never made the main event, there was an accepted legal process whereby the vows of such non-combatants could be redeemed in kind, usually in the form of cash or property, credited direct into Vatican coffers. Many landed gentry signed over to Rome their rights to feudal ownership in redemption: as in 1236 when Earl Richard of Cornwall sold off his woodlands, while Richard I in 1189 had allowed the transfer of some English royal castles in Scotland to the Scots king in exchange for 10,000 marks cash, millions of pounds today. The Vatican's whole revenue recovery process was tuned to a fine art so that its entire subordinate Christendom was divided into twenty-six collection areas, each staffed by a hierarchy of papal agents (Lombardy bankers) ensuring all localities under their supervision paid the appropriate contribution. Small wonder indeed that in future times Hubert was often to think he was fighting a losing battle when his Angevin overlords raided the English Treasury to fund some remote European cause in a little-heard of country. But, if you can't beat them, join them; Hubert too was to register his vow – and one day he had to cash it in.

Speaking of cash and the Crusades, the Order of the Knights Templar stood as international bankers for those who wished to redeem their Crusade vow in cash. Acting as financial intermediaries between the Vatican and those wishing to be recognized as Crusadeworthy, the London Temple church in this role became the equivalent of a modern City clearing house. A potent sign of the seniority accorded the Templars' status occurs in the preamble to the 1215 version of Magna Charta, where the Templar Order is listed immediately following the name of the papal legate Pandulf, and ahead of England's most senior peer the great William Marshal, Earl of Pembroke, and all other signatory English peers.

In fact the Templars had a substantial footprint in and around the environs of Dover Castle: their chapel ruins on the Western Heights still survive. In the Kent hinterland the pivotal HQs were at Strood, Temple Waltham, and Temple Ewell where traces of their estate management can still be discerned today. The tenants on these Templar estates carried out a multitude of tasks we would collectively today call farming; while those near coastlines also managed herring fishery businesses. In Hubert's day there were some fifty tenants at Temple Ewell at any one time.

On Henry II's death and Richard's succession in July 1189 a truce to local infighting was agreed with Philip of France for himself and Richard to go together to the Holy Land. The succession had not been straightforward. Richard's elder brother Geoffrey had died in 1186 from a serious virus infection, but he had left an infant son, Prince Arthur of Brittany, whose feudal right to succeed to the English throne was initially ignored by Richard. However, in September 1190, en route to the Holy Land, Richard stopped off in Sicily to visit his sister Joan, widow of King William II, the late Norman King of Sicily. Because Joan wouldn't agree to an inheritance arrangement in Richard's favour, Richard seized the city of Messina in retribution. The island dissolved into turmoil. A peace settlement was eventually agreed which in exchange for a considerable sum (40,000oz of gold) to further fund his Crusade, Richard was made to acknowledge that Arthur, not John, was indeed his rightful heir to the English throne, and that Richard permitted him to be married when he came of age to the daughter of the new King of Sicily, Tancred of Lecce, an illegitimate cousin of William's. Just before leaving Sicily Richard is said to have presented Tancred with a sword named Excalibur: presumably to confirm an Arthurian link. Leaving Crusaders and the mixed Sicilian population still at each other's throats, Richard carried on to the Holy Land. But when the news got back to Europe two opposing factions, one for Prince Arthur, one for Richard, immediately started to build their respective support while the two kings were absent. This situation was to have dramatic consequences for Hubert de Burgh's career.

Hubert was only on the fringe of Richard's court during the latter half of the Lionheart's reign, being in fact utilized by John more and more, so much so that in 1193 John made to Hubert a gift of the manors of Croxton (Leics.) and Sedgebrook (Lincs.) in recognition of his services rendered. With these 'feoffments' Hubert acquired a useful regular income from their lands and fees; a modest start to a career that would at its peak see him owning rich and extensive properties across at least fourteen English counties. But it is important to remember that Hubert's origin was not of 'landed gentry' baronage, so he had to make his way in a court peopled by continental aristocrats mostly from centuries-old families: nothing came to him on a plate; he had to earn his credibility, day by day. Meanwhile at court the news was dominated by accounts of the overseas battles. Hubert heard all about Richard's epic victories at Jaffa (1190) and Acre (1191), utilizing a strategic mix of siege and naval warfare techniques not seen before, to oust the Saracens and institute a Christian regime at Jerusalem. Nearer home he heard at first hand from some of the workmen back from Normandy about Richard's construction of the latest in castle design at his Château-Gaillard, built to defend the main route from Rouen to Paris. Hubert was soon to see it for himself, as he went with John to the continent in 1198. The surviving records for the following year indicate that John was taking in a tour of Normandy while his elder brother was supervising his castle improvements outside Rouen, and the same sources show Hubert with John's entourage. What his exact role was is not defined, but it was significant enough for John to allow him on 8 February 1198 to countersign a charter concerning the local trade delegations in Tinchebrai. Then, in the July, he witnessed another charter, this time in the office of chamberlain (household manager) to King John. This now made him one of the most senior people in John's personal court. In this role he would become John's closest advisor and, consequently, the one most in the know of John's intentions – or so he thought.

Meanwhile, as his castle of Châlus-Chabrol was under siege by Richard the Lionheart's forces in the evening of 11 March 1199, French crossbow marksman, Pierre Basile, from the security of his 100ft-high battlement, took careful aim down at the central character of a group of English nobles distantly assessing the castle defences. Releasing his bolt he scored a direct hit on his target – and changed the course of European history. Richard the Lionheart died on 6 April from the gangrenous infection left by Basile's bolt which had vertically pierced the King's left shoulder. The surgery of the day was helpless and indeed, in this case, made things worse: Richard suffered a long, drawn out and excruciatingly painful end. Soon panic was abroad in the Angevin homeland!

Chapter 3

John 1199–1216

1199–1202 Chamberlain and Confidant

With his staff Hubert, now as chamberlain, ran John's court for him. Maintaining records, receiving and paying cash or bills of credit to and from the English Treasury, keeping castles in repair, garrisoned and provisioned; keeping John's wardrobe in good order, organizing catering and entertaining. But Hubert was also always on the lookout for any opportunity to consolidate his own financial and political status: no 'jobs for life' existed in Angevin courts. Integrated with the above tasks came a wider, more sensitive role which included the payment and receipt of monies to and from John's personal treasure, acceptance and donation of royal gifts, and payments to military mercenaries recruited for specific actions at home or abroad. In his successful prosecution of these complex responsibilities under the most demanding of masters, and in his avoidance of the pitfalls and traps set for him by jealous native Angevins within the court, Hubert was to progress to become John's right-hand man. And it suited John to have at hand someone he felt he could trust personally and who projected an anglicized commentary on national trends and events.

Earlier, when John had received the news of his brother Richard's death, he was visiting Arthur's court in Brittany, with Hubert in his entourage. Then as (uncrowned) monarch John immediately departed south to Chinon to take control of the Angevin Treasury there. The Order of the Knights Templar also housed their treasure within its massive walls, an arrangement of Henry II's: as a fee for this responsibility Henry had granted the Order payments of one mark from every sheriff's farm in England. The payments continued until the Order's dissolution in 1312. Hubert would also in later times make use of the Templars' sophisticated banking system. On 25 April 1199 John moved on to Rouen to be installed as Duke of Normandy. After returning to England with Hubert, he received the English crown at

Westminster on 27 May 1199. Now, as King John, he made haste to cement his credibility by returning to the continent with Hubert in January 1200 to agree a truce with Philip. This temporary cessation of hostile intent – the Peace of Le Goulet – was followed by the marriage of Philip's son Louis to Blanche of Castile, John's niece. As a result of the truce Prince Arthur and his followers became even further distanced from any militant attempt on the English throne.

Marriage was in the air in the spring of 1200. Hubert set the pace in mid-April with a proposal to marry Joan, the youngest daughter of William, Earl of Devon. The match would bring him (he hoped) the Isle of Wight and the Manor of Christchurch in Hampshire. However, when the countess bore a son the clauses in the marriage agreement gave these lands to the heir, leaving Hubert with a (relatively) paltry £60 a year and the service of ten knights. Hubert moved on.

The level of personal trust John now had in his chamberlain was illustrated by Hubert being chosen to lead an embassy in June 1200 to explore the possibilities of John marrying the daughter of the King of Portugal. However, as this political party clambered across the Pyrenees, and in a typically Angevin 'seat of the pants' reversal of decision, John found it more politically expedient to choose a bride nearer home and accordingly betrothed himself to and wed Isabella of Angoulême at Chinon on 26 August 1200. This upset several major players in Poitou, including the powerful Lusignan family which had expected Isabella to form part of their plans. So Hubert, on being recalled at the end of November, found a new wife in John's household, strife in the continental kingdom, and the hoped-for Portuguese union not seeing the light of day. After Hubert's return John presented him with a menu of homeland safety measures to be put in hand; at the same time, keeping his right-hand man sweet, he authorized Hubert as sheriff of Hereford, and later of Dorset and Somerset. His continual underlying worry was of a border incursion by Welsh forces while he was away on the continent so, in reward for his well-organized management of his household, John gave Hubert the service of 100 knights to further bolster the security of the Welsh border. Even more importantly to Hubert he was made castellan of the vital three-castle group which ever after became synonymous as 'The Three Castles of the Justiciar', namely Grosmont, Skenfrith, and Whitecastle, all in Gwent and commanding the most sensitive southern approaches to the Welsh kingdom from England. In modern times each castle has been comprehensively researched and maintained, and their role in both Hubert's and the locality's life is explained in the excellent presentation by the Welsh Historic Monuments Office CADW.[1] By means of this gift John, during his travels across the Channel in 1201–1202, entrusted to his chamberlain the security of a sizeable portion of the kingdom.

Hubert de Burgh was a born administrator, a skill that fitted well with the aspirations of John's court in these opening years of a new century. All modern historians agree that the initiative for a co-ordinated management of government records – Chancery, Treasury, Exchequer – dates indisputably from the first years of John's reign, created most likely at his behest and brought into being by a chosen team of men with paperwork management skills akin to Hubert's ('information management' in modern terms). An educated guess would infer that much of the smooth running of the newly emergent national accounting system could be credited to Hubert's personal abilities, allied to his rising seniority, as yet barely out of his late twenties. For much of the present period that Hubert was in England he was to be found networking and dealing at Westminster, where clear evidence emerges of his inexorable rise and rise by his first appearance in the records of 1201 as a baron of the Exchequer: his early years spent amassing financial knowledge and contacts were now paying off. The English Exchequer formed the Westminster fiscal control room of the Angevin kingdom; a seat then at its famous chequered cloth table might be equated to a seat on the Bank of England's board today. As an Exchequer baron Hubert was automatically exempt from paying scutage tax. Medieval scutage was a tax meaning 'shield money'; a sum to be paid by tenants-in-chief of an estate financially commuting their obligation to provide military forces in support of the monarch. It was roughly 20 shillings per knight on the sheriff's estate and was recovered by the tenant-in-chief from his tenants. Hubert received substantial amounts of this tax from his growing number of county shrievalties but now had no obligation to pass it on to the Exchequer; instead it became a steady source of supplementary income, probably no less than 10 per cent of his total. Additionally, as an Exchequer baron, Hubert was required to account to the King for the finances of his county property holdings only when and if the King requested the figures: for all other sheriffs it was a mandatory six-monthly tax return. Hubert was not quick to jog John's memory when his own return was becoming overdue.

His appointments as county sheriff put him in charge of the royal castles of the county, as opposed to those castles owned and held by private families. Under his authority as castellan Hubert became entitled to collect taxes and revenues due from landholders within the royal demesnes and to receive any fines levied by shire courts. In practice his seniority enabled him to appoint his own staff to take care of the on-the-ground administration of his growing collection of castles, shrievaltys and forfeited estates. In 1202–3 alone he amassed this astonishing list of civil ranks, properties, and other income sources – sheriff of Dorset and Somerset, Berkshire, Cornwall, and Herefordshire; custodian of Corfe Castle; castellan of the castles of Launcester and Wallingford; custodian of the baronies of Beauchamp and Dunster; receiver of the lands of Emma de Beaufoy in Ludham, Nottinghamshire, and at Creake, Norfolk; custodian of the estates forfeit of Alan, Count of Tregueir, in Saham, Cambridgeshire, Aylesham, Norfolk, and Waltham, Lincolnshire. So at this time, while Hubert stayed in the highest court circles, he received increasingly lucrative dues from these lands. Where royal lands anywhere in the county fell to the custody of a 'minor' due to an incumbent's decease, then the management of them automatically defaulted to the royal household, with the King deciding which courtier he would favour with the care (and income) of these lands until the minor came of age and assumed control. Such sources of income could last for anything up to twenty years; and if the minor died before reaching majority, the custodial landholder could pursue a legal case for his personal retention of the estate. Hubert used his influential position, quite self-servingly most times, to receive such 'honours' through his career, some for only a few months, but most for many years from this time onwards, and many of these 'honours' were in his home counties of Norfolk, Lincolnshire, Essex, and Cambridgeshire. With his acquisition of these various lands also came some legal responsibility for the welfare of the local people earning a living, manual or administrative, living on them. Hubert looked after those who served him well and made many friendships, his principal ones being Luke his chaplain, and chaplain to Eustace, Bishop of Ely, who was to be at his side, politically and very often physically, for much of Hubert's life; Laurence of St Alban's, his legal clerk and occasional amanuensis; and not least Matthew Paris, another St Alban's monk, lifetime friend and, to a large extent, Hubert's original biographer.

Luke, Hubert's chaplain, probably knew him better than anyone, and he received many 'preferments' through Hubert's influence. When Hubert's brother Geoffrey vacated the archdeaconry of Norwich in 1225 the vacancy was filled by Luke; previously (1223) he had been promoted to the chancellorship of Lichfield cathedral. A London benefice came his way also with the deanery of St Martin's le Grand. Early in 1224 he was found a place as Treasurer of the King's chamber. In between all these responsibilities he went on to be a canon at Salisbury cathedral. He seemed to have peaked with promotion to the archbishopric of Dublin in 1230, but documentary delays kept him at Hubert's side until 1231 when he went to his archdiocese and become right-hand man to Hubert's brother Richard.

Hubert's 'honours' mentioned above were all working agricultural fraternities; they had seen their overlords change at regular intervals, but as tenants they kept their heads down and continued in 'the noiseless tenor of their way'. At this time small townships were developing across the country, their inhabitants clearing woodlands and heath for crop and animal husbandry. By 1300 it is estimated that across England there were some 700 emerging town communities, a substantial indicator of peasantry effort to improve their lot – in the year 1100 only about 100 'towns' had been formed. Some rural areas also had relatively heavy industry: by 1212 the West Country was mining a million pounds of tin annually. Also the ports were regularly shipping out the fleeces of 12 million sheep raised on farms such as those Hubert counted in his 'honours'. It was to his advantage to see that his tenants were looked after.

Chapter 4

1202–1207 Castellan in Conflict

During 1201 John had been flexing his military muscles across Normandy in response to the threat of a new alliance being forged between the disaffected Lusignan family and the adherents to Prince Arthur's cause as rightful heir to the English throne. John himself had created most of his own problems with his marriage to Isabella, heiress to the great Angoulême lands, and hoped for bride-to-be of Hugh de Lusignan. Hubert had initially gone in 1201 with John's forces but was returned by the King to England in the December of that year with specific orders to assume command as castellan of Dover, its castle being the most strategic defence point of the realm in commanding the movement of all vessels taking the short sea route to and from the continent. Because a three-way exchange of castellanships involving royal castles in Cornwall and Oxfordshire was a necessary preliminary to Hubert's acquisition of Dover, he could not take possession of the fortress until 21 March 1202.[1] However, from that day forward, Dover Castle was ever to remain associated with the name and reputation of Hubert de Burgh. During the following month the barons of the Cinque Ports were also ordered to adhere to the command of the new castellan and Constable of Dover, his orders to them now carrying the King's authority. So was initiated the role later to be assumed by and identified with the Lords Warden of the Cinque Ports.

While Hubert was in England and specifically involved with this administration of Dover, these few months in the year 1202 seem the most likely time for his foundation there of the Maison Dieu, or Hospital of St Mary. Although shortly to demonstrate his mettle as a soldier who led from the front, Hubert was in other ways a man of notable ecclesiastical benevolence. Although inevitably altered with the passage of time, Hubert's building survives in Dover to this day. Its original role was to cater for pilgrims passing through Dover to and from the continent, its foundation charter defining it as: 'For the maintenance of the poor and infirm, and pilgrims.'[2] Managed by a Master and a mix of lay brethren and sisters, apart from short-stay pilgrims travelling to and from the continent, it also took in the sick-poor and some destitute soldiers as pensioners. Today we would call Maison Dieu a charity, receiving as it did bequests, donations, and benefactions from a wide range of philanthropic sources. It was especially fortunate in respect of Hubert's contributions; being a senior courtier, over the years he settled a series of extremely valuable charters upon the hospital. It was largely these which enabled it to ride out the Dissolution storms of later centuries and so live on to present times as a permanent and much cared for legacy of Hubert's generosity.

The Maison Dieu internal discipline was strict but fair. Having first taken an oath of obedience to the Master on entering, the most able inmates were expected to work with the staff helping with the in-house daily work. This was centred around the essential utilities of the kitchen, dairy, bake-house, washroom, and brew house. Typical daily food would be a meat pottage, fish on Fridays, a 10oz loaf at 1/2d and a ¾ pint of ale. At harvest time all hands were expected to join in to bring the crop in, the following celebrations often involving a 'harvest goose'. The hospital gardens were also maintained where fruit, vegetables and herbs, both culinary and medicinal, were grown. Probably too a small farm animal plot set aside for goats, sheep, chickens and the like, to be tended. The inmates usually ate at a common round table in the main room. On Sundays they might attend a communal drink gathering at which the Master gave each one a penny, the inmates then gave a farthing back for the ale jug. Feast days were held at Christmas, Twelfth Day and Easter when inmates might have meat, fish, spiced milk, oatmeal, spiced cakes, bread and ale. Prayers and saying of psalters for the hospital's founders and benefactors closed the evening. The actual collection of monetary alms was the preserve of the male brethren, with documented accounts and general management reports rendered to the local mayor at set intervals. Hubert's parting gift to Dover – The Maison Dieu ('God's House') – opened for business in 1203.

By mid-August 1202 Hubert had been recalled to John's service in Normandy: he would not see England again for some years.[3] At the time he was getting himself down to the Channel, some twenty or so Lusignan adherents to Prince Arthur's cause in England had got themselves into trouble. They were imprisoned in Corfe Castle and decided to starve themselves to death there rather than submit to John's rule which they considered illegal. Technically they were right. It was to cope with such examples as this of the 'Arthur effect' now raging pandemically across Normandy that saw Hubert on the next available boat. As his crossing cost 40 shillings paid for by the sheriff of Sussex, Hubert enjoyed a relatively comfortable crossing on a typical go-anywhere Cinque Ports cog, though as now Constable of Dover, he probably shared the Captain's cabin. At the same time he had no illusions about the dangers towards which he was heading. On every trip to the Continent, and especially this one, his travelling chest held his armour, sword, mail and helm: maybe too a flask of Bordeaux and, always, his rosary. He found John with his Angevin forces embattled against the French King. Philip had managed to put together an alliance of the influential Lusignan family together with adherents of Prince Arthur. Consequently, the combined rebel power of the provinces of Poitou, Anjou, Maine and Touraine, backed by the French army, was now heading into John's inherited lands. Their initial target was Mirabeau Castle where John's mother, Queen Eleanor, was besieged. But on the rare occasions when John got his priorities right he was unstoppable, and so it was at Mirabeau. His forces, including Hubert as a senior commander, totally routed the siege force, freed Eleanor, captured the 15-year-old Prince Arthur, three of the Lusignan brothers, and took prisoner a significant number of the rebels. John then sent Hubert, with a large force, on to Falaise to assume the castellanship of its mighty fortress: Hubert took with him Arthur, together with Geoffrey and Hugh Lusignan. On John's orders he was to defend Falaise against any force. But what was going to happen next inside Falaise Castle could not have been made up!

A month or so later Hubert received at Falaise a notification from John's headquarters at Rouen to the effect that 'no treaty of peace could be considered while Arthur was alive', and that John had been counselled to approve the proposal that Arthur be mutilated in a manner which would make it impossible for him to reign. Blinding and emasculation were decided upon at Rouen. The Welsh annalist of Margam Abbey proposes the following consequence through his contacts with the local populace at the time:

Some courtiers of the King, seeing that the Breton people were alarmed about the capture of lord Arthur, and that no peace treaty could be created while he still lived, told the king that he order the noble prince be deprived of eyes and genitalia and so be unable to rule, so the unruly Breton attacks then cease and the king John's rule renewed. And so, in exasperation from the continuing attacks and insults, he sent three of his close companions to go to Falaise and carry out this act of barbarism. Two of them, turned and fled the court, unable to comprehend such savagery against the young prince, but the third came to the castle and found Arthur, manacled and in the protection of Hubert. When the details of his mission were given to Hubert and the guards of soldiers, great lamentation broke out amongst them, being protective of the young prince. Arthur collapsed in terror. But he then rose up and violently attacked John's knight waiting to carry out the sentence shouting 'My lords, for God's love, give me just the time to take my vengeance upon this criminal ere he tears out my eyes, for then he will be the last I see in this age!' The guard of knights stepped between the prince and his executioner and, on Hubert's order, threw out the man from John's court. Arthur was much lightened by this action. Hubert, now thinking to preserve the king's integrity, kept Arthur from being harmed in any way, thinking that in time the king would regret his edict and vilify the person who had carried out the cruel command. He thought it was an edict born of fury and not of justice. So to find peace with king John and to stop the Bretons' insurgency, he had it divulged in the castle and the Falaise province that Arthur had died from his wounds. This was the news for the two weeks, with the funeral bell for Arthur being tolled in the churches. A sack of his clothes was distributed to a hospital of lepers. It was also said that his body was now at the Cistercian abbey of St André, and there interred. But this caused the Bretons to be more enraged saying they would not rest from attacking the king of England who had committed this crime upon his nephew and their lord. So Hubert found it necessary to discount the rumour he had started, and to proclaim that Arthur was still alive and unharmed so that the Bretons might cease their lamentation and attacks. When John found out all this he was not displeased his order had been disobeyed.

If this account is taken at face value, then in saving Arthur, and probably himself, Hubert had displayed an astute understanding of John's character – he was perhaps the only contemporary who had learned to read John's methods of thought, John realized that Hubert had successfully defused a critical political situation, and from which no-one (so far) had emerged as losers: but even Hubert could not completely quell John's innate murderous streak. Consequently he could make no opposition to John when he visited Falaise on 30 January 1203 to take Arthur away with him back to Rouen Castle. At the same time in an act of inconceivable short-sightedness, John ordered Hubert to release the Lusignan brothers, presumably to appease Philip and his continuously threatening army. The pitiful Prince Arthur (rightful heir to the English throne) was never seen alive again outside Rouen Castle. Another contemporary recorded the outcome as he knew it:

> After king John had captured Arthur and kept him alive in prison for some time, at length, at the castle of Rouen after dinner on the Thursday before Easter [3 April 1203] when he was drunk, he slew him with his own hand, and tying a heavy stone to the body cast it into the Seine. It was discovered by a fisherman in his net, and being dragged to the bank and identified, was taken for secret burial, in fear of the tyrant, to the prior of Bec.[4]

Historians have always found this passage of events surrounding Prince Arthur's murder a conundrum of inexplicable actions. Hubert was a merciless man when he personally was sent on any specific task to achieve a settlement, whatever the circumstances. So why did he not step up to the mark on this occasion? John was always going to eliminate the threat to his throne from Arthur and his following: it was just a case of how and when. And Hubert must have known this. What neither Hubert nor the King could anticipate was what would be the outcome of such an action? Hubert could have been well pleased when John arrived and took away Arthur – with him went any responsibility Hubert could have for the outcome. But none of this stopped William Shakespeare from letting the gory facts get in the way of a good plot for his play *The Life and Death of King John*: consequently Hubert's supposed role as villainous accomplice in this unique royal felony was set in type forever thereafter.

Now the sickening rumours that swept across Europe could not be denied: the genie – that John had personally murdered Arthur – was out of the bottle. Total war now became inevitable. Hastily trying to assemble a virtually hopeless defence of his Angevin lands, John ordered his two most trusted castellans into the region's two most strategically important fortresses. Gerard d'Athies, seneschal of Touraine, went to command Loches, while Hubert installed himself at Chinon in the Loire valley – defending the Angevin Treasury. He spent that summer of 1203 consolidating his defences with his second in command, Philip de Ulecotes, so that by the winter, when John finally crept back to England on 5 December, Chinon was as impregnable as its commanding situation and resources could make it. Only token help for the two castellans would be forthcoming from John, the rebellious barony saw to that: 'why should they offer any help to someone now known across Europe by the nickname "Softsword"!' As a sidelight, these punitive taxation demands by John on his populace at this time gave rise to the 'Robin Hood' legend. Interestingly, the legend was to take more substantive form later in 1225 when a Yorkshire-born sheriff, Eustace of Lowdham, confiscated the chattels of an outlaw named Robert (Robin?) Hood. The same person was also known as Robert of Wetherby. Eustace, then acting sheriff of Nottingham, captured the outlaw and beheaded him. But was it Robin or Robert whose body hung in chains in the following weeks?

Meanwhile in Chinon, Hubert expected to hear nothing more from his fractious monarch; as Richard the Lionheart had once commented, 'My brother John is not the man to win lands by force if there is anyone at all to oppose him.' In any event, the final battle lines were soon to be put in place by Philip who was to throw everything (literally) into this golden opportunity to overrun large swathes of the Angevin kingdom. It wasn't much noticed at the time, but when John had hotfooted it back to England that December he was accompanied by another refugee Frenchman, Peter des Roches of Touraine clinging clam-like to John's retinue. This mercurial illegal immigrant would spend the rest of his life in England and, with his junior partner Peter de Rivallis, would become Hubert's Nemesis. As the imminent fragmentation of his kingdom was about to start across the Channel, John chose to distance himself from it all (and Hubert and Gerard) to take time out to show he wasn't all bad by authorizing in 1203 the foundation of a Cistercian monastic abbey at Beaulieu in the New Forest, on a site that used to be a royal hunting lodge. It was a token appeasement by John for trespass by his forest bailiffs on Cistercian lands a few years earlier: today much still survives at Beaulieu from John's time.

Philip's campaign started in earnest in March 1204 when Richard the Lionheart's favourite castle, Château Gaillard at Les Andelys, commanding the main road from Paris to Rouen, fell within a fortnight: the Lionheart's supposedly state-of-the-art defences hopelessly outdated by the latest in French siege artillery. John's released Lusignan brothers gave Philip a further easy ride by negotiating the surrender of Poitiers, Chatellerault, and Chauvigny, so handing to Philip control of the provinces of Maine, Anjou and Brittany. Almost as a formality Philip then marched into Normandy which completely capitulated by the end of June. The French king now had in place an impregnable northern bulwark under his command enabling him to safely turn his forces southwards towards the regions defended by the fortresses of Loches and Chinon. Philip knew the reputations of the men awaiting him and he expected no surrender from either of them. He was not to be disappointed. Chinon Castle is the sole building on top of an isolated granite outcrop some hundred feet high. At the base of the rock face lived (and still does) its small local community: the citizens' environment limited by the rock to one side and by the River Vienne to the other. The castle fortifications sprawl over half a mile along the top of the outcrop, which itself has a ravine feature dividing its centre. The castle keep and main defences were surrounded by continuous curtain walling which abutted a sheer drop on three sides. The fourth side, with the castle's main gate, was reached only over a drawbridge across the ravine. Castle buildings of lesser significance occupied the lower side from the ravine outside the gate.

By September 1204 Philip had reinforced and increased his army following the northern campaign: now he felt confident enough to take on Loches and Chinon: but things didn't go to plan. With both castles having river as well as multiple wall defence systems, to Philip's annoyance he had achieved little more than damaging only their most outlying walls after a month's bombardment. His commander Dreux de Mello had received heavy losses from Gerard d'Athies' spirited defence at Loches; while at Chinon, although the French infiltrated the lower ward, Hubert's skilled use of his crossbowmen firing their bolts from his battlements across the ravine into the attacking force, laid waste considerable numbers of Philip's men. The crossbow had developed into a highly lethal offensive weapon and the bolts fired by Hubert's men had the latest refinement. Their feathered flights were not fixed at right angles to the shaft (like a dart) but instead were twisted slightly around the shaft helically. When released the bolt thus spun in flight – as does a rifle bullet – so achieving much increased penetrating force, greater accuracy, and longer range. The French, of course, had similar weapons, but having to fire them upwards at the Chinon walls made personal safety at the same time impossible. Consequently with his archers firing downwards from their castle parapets into the lower ward at Chinon, Hubert's defensive skills in using his archers to best effect left large numbers of Philip's men dead around the castle approaches, or fatally infected with blood poisoning.[5] The first round had gone to the English; however the two castellans had no illusions about the seriousness of the position in which John had left them. They could withstand Philip only as long as their supplies, military and humanitarian, lasted out: and neither was holding their breath for any imminent arrival of a relieving force from across the Channel. Consequently, Gerard and Hubert occupied themselves in making good the autumn campaign damage to their fortresses before settling into a long winter wait. John, meanwhile, knew too well that much of his kingdom was at risk if he did nothing to help, and so began putting in place preparations for an expeditionary invasion force next May. But he had reckoned without the excellent secret network of French spies in England. Forewarned of John's intentions and deadline, Philip was able to trump him by sending his much augmented and heavily armed force south in April 1205.

By mid-May the very latest in Philip's siege artillery came trundling over the horizon in large numbers, to the considerable apprehension of the defenders of Loches. Philip had at his disposal the cutting edge siege technology of the day in the form of massively powerful catapults which could project far heavier missiles over far greater distances and heights than had previously been possible. He practised with them against Loches first and before the end of May Gerard d'Athies was forced to capitulate, his castle in ruins around him. With his techniques now fine-tuned, Philip moved up the Loire valley to Chinon where Hubert awaited his best efforts, already aware through his own spy network of the Loches capitulation. Having held out through the winter of 1204, the prospect of defending the now depleted castle against most of the French army and its awesome artillery made even Hubert certain of the inevitability of the outcome. But at the same time he would have wryly smiled thinking how the French king had complimented his castellanship in being forced to devote the majority of his army and siege engines f r a year and more to overcome his determined and uncompromising defence of this one fortress. Hubert de Burgh was held in high regard by Phillip, King of France. It took Philip well into June to force Chinon into submission: it was never surrendered by Hubert. At the end, on 23 June, the eve of St John the Baptist's day, the surviving defenders burnt all their remaining supplies to prevent their use by the French and, in a 'last hurrah' charge with Hubert and Philip de Ulecotes side by side in the lead, they ran out over the rubble to take on the French in one final desperate hand-to-hand skirmish. 'They fought courageously to the point of death!' recorded one chronicler of this epic battle, accounts of which were told and retold for many years afterwards in the courts on both sides of the Channel. Hubert was very badly injured in the final mêlée, but Philip on capturing him sent him personally for care, recuperation (and ransom) to the coastal château of Renaud de Dammartin, count of Boulogne; there Hubert was to stay recovering slowly until his ransom was negotiated, and his health allowed his return to England.

The 35-year-old had survived months of tension and stress: taking mail and armour on and off, his leather gambeson continually encrusted with dried sweat and blood; always with sword to hand; unable to relax his supervision of the fortress and its occupants for a moment – then finishing with a winner-takes-all fight to the death. A period of recuperation by the sea at Boulogne, having bed rest, his wounds treated, regular meals, and with a compliant custodian, was an interlude that Hubert probably anticipated with some congeniality. It was during this enforced stay at Boulogne that news came to him of the death of his elder brother William who had been John's man in Ireland since 1185. In 1205 John, to buttress his own plans, conceded two thirds of the Connaught dominion to the Irish O'Connor family; in so doing he undermined all of William's achievements at peace. How much this betrayal contributed to William's death we are left to wonder.

With the fall of Chinon and Loches Philip gained control of Touraine and so consolidated his hold on all the former Angevin lands north of Poitou and Aquitaine; in time he would see Hubert return there, but in a much more senior role than prisoner of war. Meantime Hubert had in this campaign cemented his reputation, both as a fixer and as a fighter.

Chapter 5

1207–1213 From Scapegoat to
Seneschal of Poitou

John was unwanted in his realm. His Angevin nobles had seen the loss of their hereditary property to the French King, while the English barons found the whole continental adventure an expensive distraction from the government of England. Implicitly Hubert de Burgh was held to be at fault by John in allowing Chinon to fall and so effectively surrendering to Philip the key defensive barrier of the Loire valley; from here Philip could strengthen his control of the newly acquired north and threaten the still independent southern provinces. Hubert, convalescing in Boulogne and computing his ransom arrangements, could not respond to any of John's accusations, he could only watch and wait as he learned that the ever-rapacious monarch, during October 1205, had confiscated much of his lands and property and, for the most part, turned these assets into cash for his own pecuniary purposes. The King's programme of confiscation continued unabated until the spring of 1206, but on many of these property transfer transactions John overrode the law of the land: this Hubert would in due course exploit to his ultimate advantage.

There seems nowhere to exist any acceptable reason why John decided to vilify and punish Hubert so ferociously. Hubert had used his skills as a military tactician to the full, as the swathes of French dead around Chinon Castle attested; and Philip had been forced to conduct a very expensive campaign over large regions of his kingdom during a long period of time. In the taking of Hubert's property simply because it was what he wanted to do, John was riding a coach and horses through the pertaining laws. These laws allowed the confiscation of baronial property only on the grounds of a treasonable act settled before a court of law and the baron convicted as a result, or a baron's death with no heir. Neither of these circumstances existed in Hubert's case: John was guilty of exceeding his regnal powers.

Hubert he replaced in the office of chamberlain with Geoffrey de Neville. The erstwhile refugee Peter des Roches didn't miss out either; John granted him the vastly wealthy bishopric of Winchester in September 1205. This uninvited battling bishop came to be seen as more familiar with the castle parapet than with the cathedral pulpit. Meanwhile the survivors of the Chinon battle had started to arrive back at court and John had been forced to accept the facts they recounted describing Hubert's heroism and that of his comrade in arms, Gerard d'Athies, from Loches – but Hubert himself was to remain incarcerated at Boulogne until the February of 1207. During his sojourn with the Duke of Boulogne, Hubert would certainly have become aware of the existence of another factor which was destined to change his life forever – Plantagenet pirate and Cinque Ports vandal, Eustace the Monk. But who exactly was this potentially life-changing villain: this 'Eustace the Monk' who in future times would meet Hubert in other battles on which also hinged the fate of Europe?

Medieval legend about Eustace – infamous then, unknown now – both amplifies and obscures his reputation, but most of what we know today is derived from a French epic saga *The Romance of Eustace the Monk*. Composed probably about 1230, the anonymous author accords his hero something of the status of his contemporary, Robin Hood. But Eustace never robbed the rich to give to the poor: Eustace just robbed everybody! Although the *Romance* heavily overlays Eustace's life with mysticism, an undercurrent of verifiable historical fact is discernible about this unique medieval character. His birthplace has generally been agreed to have been at the village of Courset, about ten miles south-east of Boulogne. His actual residence was most likely the Château de Course a little further away, which he inherited from his father, Bauduin Busquet. During his early years there the young Eustace is described in local accounts of the times as having achieved the status of 'chevalier de Boulenois', implying some military training equivalent to that of a knight. But it was not long before Eustace set off to explore the world outside the forests of Boulogne. He seems to have travelled south initially, and almost certainly spent some time on the southern French coast, probably in the Marseilles locality. At this, one of the busiest of Mediterranean ports, Eustace seems to have started to accumulate a practical hands-on scholarship in shipping and seamanship. For all his faults Eustace was, for long after his passing, recognized as the most skilled of all medieval mariners in that most unforgiving of seascapes, the English Channel. At Marseilles he is very likely to have worked as a crew member, voyaging perhaps even to the Middle East, as well as to the French Atlantic coast ports. His later maritime Channel exploits certainly demonstrated a familiarity with shipping practices generally found in the Mediterranean.

Marseilles was also the premier Crusades shipping point, being the midway stopping off point between northern Europe and the Holy Land. (The Knights Templar, it will be recalled, who organized much of the Crusades' logistics, based their pilgrim fleet at Marseilles.) There was too another possibility that Eustace found attractive in the Order of Knights Templar – their well known links with superstition and sorcery. Eustace always liked to have an edge over his opponents and the acquisition of a necromancy skill, apparently used with some effect by the Templars, would certainly be a useful tool in the armoury of this militant mariner. Thus we find that the chronicler of the *Romance* tells us that Eustace travelled on from France to Spain where he is said to have spent most of a year in Toledo 'learning the techniques and arts of deception'. Although the story-teller offers no specific source for this legendary period of Eustace's life, Toledo was certainly infamous as the leading European school offering courses of formal instruction in the black arts. The other aspect of Templar life which perhaps Eustace took on board as useful training was the Order's avowed monkish origins, being defined in early sources as 'Brothers of Jerusalem, Knights of the Temple of Solomon'. There appears to be no other explanation why such a callous and coarse character as Eustace should next be found impersonating as a Black Monk at the Benedictine abbey of St Samer, in his own backyard, only a couple of miles from Courset. But such an imbalance of piety and his inborn piratical nature was never going to last long and Eustace was in due course off again on his travels, having only stayed long enough both to entirely upset the abbey's contemplative routine, and also to take with him everything there that had a resale value. Any influence monastic life may have had on Eustace was short-lived; by the year 1200 he had gathered together his own gang of cut-throat mercenaries and had started on a career as a kind of personal 'bouncer' for the local lord, Renaud de Dammartin, Count of Boulogne. Largely concerned with what he could get out of the arrangement, Eustace (now called 'the Monk') was to be careless with the responsibilities that Renaud conferred upon him.

Renaud himself was a noble with some influence, having charge of the administration of Boulogne, a premier French port facing the short sea route to England. Although nominally doing homage to the French King, Philip II, Renaud was always a chancer. His loyalty tended to waver as political opportunities emerged from the hesitant alliances frequently brokered between the several nearby countries having Channel coasts. In 1197 he had sided with Richard the Lionheart and invaded some French provinces to aid his cause. Then the following year he renewed a peace treaty with Philip, only to rethink his position in 1199 on John's accession when he made an alliance with the English. He was again on the rebound in 1200, when he acquired Eustace's 'skills', because John had settled a temporary truce with Philip. To keep Renaud onside Philip had gifted to him the county of Dammartin for three thousand silver marks, together with the Norman counties of Varenne, Aumale and Mortain. In exchange Renaud gave Philip the strategically important castle of Mortemer, so allowing the French King a gateway into Normandy. According to the *Romance* chronicler, while in Renaud's pay, Eustace was responsible for several questionable actions concerning his gang and the various forces of both Philip and Renaud when they happened to encounter one another in the miles of dense Marais-Royal forests and marshlands surrounding Boulogne. In every action Eustace came off best. By 1204 Renaud had had enough; he declared Eustace and his gang outlaws and set to hunting them out of the forest. But Eustace and his polyglot adherents escaped up to the coast and there by seaborne means continued with coastal raids and pitiless assaults upon anyone or anywhere that was found to be in any way indefensible.

The onset of Eustace the Monk's piratical actions along the Channel coincided with the period that saw King John lose most of his inherited Angevin lands to Philip. Also lost to the French were the Channel Islands. In England John, considering his survival, had become aware that Eustace might be able to do some dirty work for him: both men ('it takes one to know one') were not too dissimilar in finding a means that justified an end. By November 1205 Eustace had inveigled himself into John's court clique and gained his confidence as a mariner so much so that John, according to the official court records, supplied Eustace with thirty galleys and sent him off to retake the Channel Islands from the French. This Eustace carried out, annihilating the defending force of the castellan Romeral, with a ferocity that is still noted in the modern history of the islands. In the words of the *Romance*, 'There was nothing left to burn either in castle or manor.' John's reward was to give Eustace lands in Swaffham, Norfolk (including some he had confiscated from the homeland of the captive and helpless Hubert de Burgh).

The legend of Eustace the Monk is inextricably bound up with the fortunes of the Channel Islands for, apart from 'liberating' them from the French, he used Sark particularly as the base for his piratical raiding during the next decade along the length and breadth of the Channel. After retaking them for John he is recorded in November 1205 as bringing back to England a substantial treasure which (after quietly abstracting his share) he was told by John to take to the Cinque port of Sandwich and hand over to the use of William de Wrotham, Archdeacon of Taunton, who had responsibility for seventeen of John's fifty-one royal galleys laid up in various ports around the south and west coasts of England and southern Ireland. During this period Eustace did enough to keep him in John's good books and so allowing the piracy, of which the Cinque Ports mariners were bearing the brunt, to pass without official comment. Winchelsea and Rye, both gifted in 1085 to the absentee Norman landlord the Abbot of Fecamp, were favourite targets of Eustace. The *Romance* states that for this exploit John rewarded Eustace with a 'palace' in London, but no evidence exists to support this. However, it is more likely that the *Romance* is correct in making the Sussex Cinque Port of Winchelsea most closely associated with Eustace's activities while on the English King's payroll. It is certainly on record that Eustace often used the battle cry *Vincenesel*, 'Winchelsea', during his attacks on the Channel shipping, often against Cinque Ports' vessels. Up to the year 1210 Eustace continued to combine his operations out of his Channel Islands base with various approved ventures on behalf of John, even though some of his piracy raids on French vessels and ports were returned with invasions of the islands by the French. Over some four or five years Eustace fought against all comers, in the process alienating most of the peoples bordering both sides of the Channel. Indeed, the English records for this period show Eustace as needing safe conduct passes issued to him by John personally each time he wished to visit English soil.

To conclude, the *Romance* goes on to describe a later (May 1213) successful attack made on the port of Damme where Philip was in the process of assembling a fleet to invade England. It was put together by the alliance described above and led by William Longsword, John's illegitimate brother. Although Philip lost many ships in the attack, he set fire to the remainder at their moorings to prevent them being towed away by Longsword's sailors. Renaud de Dammartin escaped Philip's pursuing force by the skin of his teeth. Philip laid the blame for the disaster on Eustace as his senior naval advisor for the lax security at the harbour at Damme, allowing the attack to happen. But he couldn't get enough proof for the charge to stick; Eustace had acquired years of skill in the avoidance of being held to account for his nefarious activities – so on this occasion he once again lived to fight another day. A revealing illumination of Eustace's Europe-wide reputation occurs at this time in the official records. The papal legate, Cardinal Guaolo, sent to discuss with Philip the political fall-out of a possible invasion of England had, as a prerequisite formality, asked Philip for a safe conduct pass through his kingdom. A translation of Philip's reply was,

Through our land I shall willingly furnish you safe-conduct; but if by chance you happen to fall into the hands of Eustace the Monk or any other of Louis' men, who guard the sea-routes, do not blame me if any harm befalls you.

Even the Pope had to tread carefully with Eustace!

The Cinque Ports mariners, especially those of the major port of Winchelsea, were continual recipients of his raids and ravaging, but it must be said to Eustace's credit that his consummate seamanship skills enabled him to master the lethal currents and tides of the Channel in a way very few sailors before him had. In respect of Winchelsea, it should be explained that Eustace's battle cry on his forays was '*Vincenesell* …!' ('Winchelsea!') The port had been considered native Normandy soil for many decades before the Norman invasion and indeed formed a kind of back gate for the uninvited, such as Eustace, to come and go more or less as they pleased without international border restrictions. This unspoken freedom was ultimately abused in 1066. A modern author explains why:

> In 1031 Canute granted the Manor of Ramslie and its port, Old Winchelsea ('winceleseg') to the Norman abbey of Fecamp, which was under the patronage of the Dukes of Normandy. This grant was of crucial importance in the history of England. It gave the Normans a foothold on a very valuable part of the coast; it is possible that without the possession of Ramslie, Duke William's invasion of England would have failed, and the future history not only of England but of Western Europe would have been very different. Winchelsea was already a port of considerable importance in the 11th century and its loyalty to its Norman overlords brought it further prosperity.[1]

A century later the port was still under the administration of the abbey as evidenced by an agreement of 1130–01 between the Abbot, Henry I and Henry Count of Eu, for the right of 'stalls and pontage' at Winchelsea. The abbot was to have half the money taken, and the King and count were to share the remaining half between them.[2] Small wonder that the Cinque Ports mariners of this era were continually volatile in their adherence to the prima facie rulers of their ports, who exercised their authority from both sides of the Channel at the same time.

All these events concerning Eustace the Monk and his piratical Channel raids would certainly have become known to Hubert during his recuperation at Boulogne, as too would have Renaud de Danmartin's aspirations to form an alliance at some future time with the Brabants and Hollanders to oppose the French King's rampant land-grabbing policy. These various insights would in the not too distant future prove invaluable to Hubert on his return to power, but for the present he continued his enforced stay at Boulogne – on the receiving end of some complex ransom negotiations.

Ransoming captives was a lucrative and recognized business in medieval times and, while a comparison with the modern football transfer market comes to mind, it was not dissimilar in having complex rules and values according to the relative prestige and seniority of the hostage, together with timescales and conditions, all factors to be mutually agreed by the countries concerned. It was quite common for a couple of lesser value hostages to be offered as part-exchange in value for the release of a single captive of individually higher value. But in general the desired outcome was one of cash payments, borrowed at interest for a fixed term paid to the captor to free the hostage back to his native land. In exceptional cases, such as Hubert de Burgh, the captor issued a document of safe passage to the hostage to facilitate their safe return, but for the majority the homeward journey after ransom payment was made at their own risk with the real possibility of recapture by a rival faction and another ransom procedure being invoked.

Hubert's ransom after nearly two years' confinement was being negotiated by his gaoler Renaud de Dammartin with the English Exchequer, and on 6 February 1207, the Exchequer was ordered to pay to middle-man William de Chayo 300 marks pledged to him by Hubert. A later payment that year from the Exchequer to Hubert was £100, half to be paid back in September, and half in the New Year. A further source that Hubert tapped was from an Arras merchant named as Martin Champs, and from whom he borrowed 1,000 marks. This enabled Hubert to leave for England in early 1207 – but he had to leave hostages with Renaud to ensure his repayments didn't fail. It would take until 1213 for Hubert to pay off the last of his ransom loans.

Back in England in spring 1207 Hubert immediately began to recover some of his confiscated properties. During the time of his captivity the truth about his heroic defence of Chinon had spread beyond the Court and a substantial and influential sympathy vote for him had accrued amongst the English rural nobility. Slowly, as he eased his way back into John's inner circle, so the land and property 'honours' the King had arbitrarily (and illegally) reverted to his own and his favourites' uses were reinstated to Hubert's benefit. Before mid-1208 he had been appointed sheriff of Lincolnshire, together with the castellanship of Sleaford and Lafford castles. It was due solely to Hubert's streetwise political zeal that he recovered his court seniority as surely and steadily as he did.

By now, in his late thirties, deeply tanned from his many years spent abroad, probably facially scarred, maybe broken-nosed from his Chinon display of leading from the front, Hubert must have presented a commanding presence at court when compared to the many career armchair courtiers, specifically the Angevin courtier-clergy who rarely left the security of their shires.

Fluent in his native English tongue, well-schooled in Norman French, capable in Latin, passable in Spanish too, a born and bred Englishman, Hubert could hold his own in discussion, debate and documentation with the best and, though these skills did not endear him to all, John nevertheless found Hubert's executive versatility and wide practical experience of use in a variety of ways. He must have radiated a tangible air of senior authority to which even John conceded a grudging respect. Hubert could entertain too, and when not in mail and armour trying to recover his King's hopeless causes, his hearts and minds skills were well evident in the social gatherings at his Westminster rooms and riverside terrace. Within a couple of years of his return he had re-attained a confident prominence again in John's entourage, was enjoying an increasing income, and had regained respect in the most influential circles at home and abroad. Hubert de Burgh in all likelihood knew John better than any other of his contemporaries did: we can only conjecture how revealing would have been any memoir Hubert could have left of this most misunderstood of all English monarchs.

In respect of the good life that Hubert enjoyed when in the capital, he and his staff had the pick of the best in price, choice and quality from the shopping streets of Westminster. The overall London population was around 60,000 people, with perhaps a third living in Westminster. To exploit their diverse tastes in comfortable living, ships from the continent, Scandinavia and the Hanseatic ports were continually arriving at the Westminster wharfs. Unloaded daily were vast quantities of peppers, ginger, cinnamon, dried fruits and spices, clothing, metal utensils and tools, foodstuffs, all meat and game, fish, simnel bread, saffron from Essex; while at the Westminster Monday fairs were sold household furnishings, ceramic pottery, jugs, and cups, candlesticks, brass pots, pewter ware, towelling and tablecloths. Anything and everything was available within the precincts of the Westminster vill for a price. The always dressed-to-impress Hubert certainly patronized the sought after services of the well-known Charing premises of John le Tailleur. In fact, he would at a later date buy into this business as part of one of his property transactions. Given the proximity of some of the richest men in the country at Westminster, it is not surprising that some records reveal tailors adding a markup twenty times the cost of their material. Often at Westminster it was family business, as with Robert and Christiana Nevill, respectively '*browderer*' and '*vestmentmaker*'. Cloth and wool trade merchants, who lived in the north of the country, were starting to migrate down to set up branches in the capital. Hubert lived at the top of his social scale – he could afford to dress the part too.

Meanwhile back in Court, John was going from bad to worse in monarchical public relations. In 1205 he had refused to recognize the papal promotion of Stephen Langton as successor to the late Hubert Walter, Archbishop of Canterbury, preferring instead his own yes-man and one-time secretary John de Grey, Bishop of Norwich. Langton had been made a cardinal in 1206, followed by his consecration to Canterbury in 1207. In March 1208, Pope Innocent III acted to resolve the situation once and for all and enforced an interdict across the entire kingdom until such time as Langton was accepted. This in effect meant that during the enforcement period the clergy were made redundant, no burials, baptisms, or marriages could receive the rites of the Roman Catholic Church, the country having been placed outside its laws. Nor could any sermons be preached or church services performed. But John took his kingdom being corporately excommunicate in his stride and, using the defence that the clergy being now out of office had no need of its property, proceeded to asset-strip the hapless clerics of their chattels, both material and pecuniary. Even the incumbents themselves were not safe from his greed as one observer describes,

> the corn of the clergy was everywhere locked up and distrained for the benefit of the revenue; the concubines of the priests and clerks were taken by the king's servants and compelled to ransom themselves at great expense.[3]

The Pope, on being made aware of John's vindictive retaliation, then passed the ultimate sanction in November 1209 making the King personally excommunicate. This was serious! Other monarchs now could use the Pope's punishment as a pretext to invade and bring John to religious submission. Some records survive to show that St Alban's Abbey suffered a worse time than most other ecclesiastical foundations. During the Papal interdiction John, for his own pecuniary means, confiscated the lands of Robert Fitzwalter over a dispute with the Abbey concerning nearby Northaw Great Wood.

Also in a token two fingers gesture to the Pope, John ordered the St Alban's abbot, John de Cella, to hold services in defiance of the edict. The abbot refused, and tried to buy John off with a bribe. John's response was 'Thanks very much' – and then he asked for more.

An interesting physical link to this time survives today in Wells Cathedral, built between *c.*1180–1239. One gang of stonemasons in 1208 were working their way along the south aisle, setting with care the identically proportioned ashlar blocks visible today – then came the excommunication described above. On being officially notified of the situation by their master-mason, the gang stayed on to concrete in place a column base and laid their foundation blocks to it; that done, they then packed up their tools and made their way to a non-religious site where working conditions (and pay) were less liable to disruption. Later, in 1229, when a completely new political authority had taken charge nationally, another gang of stonemasons returned to complete the walling from the 1208 pillar onwards. But times had also changed at the nearby Doulting quarry which had supplied stone for the cathedral from the beginning. To catch up with the many other similar contracts put on hold, the only readily available stone for the cathedral were various sized blocks cut and delivered daily on an asap basis to continue that wall along from the column – no time was available now to carefully size and cut the blocks as in twenty or so years previously. Consequently, today it is possible to stand at that wall and see (and touch) the two contrasting types of stone course eventually laid – the pre-excommunication immaculately square cut blocks then, from the pillar onwards, the random sizing of those laid as both quarry and masons worked all hours to complete the building. And it was all down to King John.

After a further passage of time during which John continued unabated in his rapacious assumed rule, the primate-elect Stephen Langton called a meeting at Winchester on 20 July 1213 at which the more subdued King was 'persuaded' that he had no rights to take land and chattels, particularly those belonging to the Church, as and when he pleased, and that he must return them. John was a bad King, Langton a uniquely brilliant diplomat – he was always going to win. Over the next months John's legal team, with much prevarication, started the process to reverse his ill-gotten gains.

Hubert was in court during these turbulent times but the part he played barely survives on documented record. That he was clearly back in some favour is marked by John deciding to award him the important and highly lucrative shrievalty of Lincolnshire in May 1208. Probably not yet as close to the King as in his days as chamberlain – and perhaps he counted himself lucky for that – he received a further favourable concession when John sent him as envoy to Poitou in 1208, and again in 1210. Hubert's usefulness to the King at this time perhaps was best served in his keeping some measure of peace in the Aquitaine dominions. Certainly he would not have wanted to be near any of the fall-out from the campaign of cruelty that John carried out in Ireland during 1210, which included the capture and starvation to death in the dungeons of Windsor Castle of the wife and son of William de Braose, a powerful Welsh border baron opposed to John's rule.

As well as seeing off insurgent threats close to home John also took measures at this time to protect his security from continental intentions against the kingdom. Between 1209 and 1212 he had constructed and launched twenty new galleys and thirty-four other support vessels from the new naval base at Portsmouth created for his Crusades voyages by his late brother Richard. An additional eight transports were built at London shipyards.[4] The galleys were intended solely for wartime, with oars to complement the speed achieved by the sail with which they were rigged, while the support transports would carry everything needed for a belligerent expedition to anywhere on the continental seaboard. This fleet, de facto an embryo Royal Navy, John kept mothballed at western and northern ports until the time was ripe for its utilization. He was in fact beefing up the fleet inherited from his brother which already comprised some fifty galleys kept in readiness at berths from East Anglia round to the Bristol Channel, including five in Irish ports. We can guess that Hubert, with his widening experience in maritime affairs, was involved in some of the procurement tasks for this fleet upgrade, but it can only be a guess, the official records remain silent on the point. Before Portsmouth, the locality of Bayonne had been the seaport of choice for galley construction to order. A master shipwright, one Galfridus of Bayonne, appears consistently as the recipient of large sums for his workshop output. Likewise, the Exchequer Rolls from *c.*1198 onwards list many orders sent to his shipyard for varying numbers of these belligerent, prow-armoured vessels of speed.

It is at this time of Hubert's resurgence at court that a woman enters his life on a more than passing basis, as from the records of 1211 he emerges as a married man. Whether it was an emotional attraction or primarily a mutually beneficent business arrangement we are left to wonder. However, Beatrice de Warrenne whose lands, known as the lordship of Wormegay, adjoined Hubert's in Norfolk, seemed eminently suitable to his ambitions, for he stood to acquire the title to her extensive and lucrative de Warrenne lands in Sussex, Yorkshire, Norfolk and Suffolk. Her late husband, the Earl William, had died leaving her sole heiress to the entire estate. In addition, Beatrice's son William, from her earlier marriage to Doon Bardolf, was still in his minority, so Hubert was able to become legal guardian to William's inheritance.[5] As always, where getting on in the world was concerned, Hubert always kept his eye on the main chance. The newly married couple were to spend little time together; in May 1212 Hubert was again sent to Poitou remaining there for the rest of the year as deputy seneschal to the incumbent Ivo de Jallia – a seneschal being a delegated ruler of the province in the King's name. By August Hubert was acting seneschal of Poitou and based at the provincial capital Niort; from there he enacted John's personal order to all the barons of the province that they must act in obedience to his seneschal's decisions.

Today we know Poitou as Poitou-Charentes, in Hubert's time it covered an area almost the size of Ireland and was bordered on its south by Aquitaine; it was therefore of vital strategic importance and John's delegation of the province to Hubert's care shows the renewed esteem in which he held his closest advisor. Hubert was confirmed as the official seneschal of Poitou on 23 August 1213, and by the end of the same year had, with Beatrice, enjoyed the birth of their son John, but what time, if any, mother and son spent with Hubert in Poitou is not known. The significance of Hubert christening his son with his King's name might not have been lost on his fellow courtiers. It was, regrettably, to be the briefest of marriages for Beatrice died towards the end of 1214. However, Hubert cannot be imagined as a devoted and attentive husband at this time. He was a hard-nosed warrior politician with little humanity of feeling when his own best interests were endangered. In another marriage in later years some softening of his character would be revealed, but for the moment he consoled himself to Beatrice's passing with the knowledge that, through his son, under the medieval inheritance law customarily known as 'the courtesy of England', Hubert was possessed of Beatrice's estates and income for his son and heir's lifetime.

Most of Hubert's problems in Poitou arose from the widespread baronial castles that littered the province; one modern authority has estimated a possible total of about ninety.[6] Most were fortified administrative centres as opposed to military fortresses for men at arms. Control of them was divided between some fifty families but these in turn were under the influence of the four principal magnates who conjointly attempted to govern affairs in Poitou – Count Hugh de Lusignan, Viscount Aimery de Thouars, Count Savaric de Mauleon, and Lord l'Archevêque de Parthenay. Political stability was never long-term; the most that Hubert could hope to achieve was to keep these principal families discussing the points at issue rather than taking arms and sides over them; and in so doing he was under orders to keep these officials sweet with the payment of large sums sent from the English Exchequer – but that wasn't bottomless!

Chapter 6

1213–1215 King John's French Farce

Intimidated by the force of international enmity that his negative attitude to the Pope had engendered, John found his position with regard to Stephen Langton's election to Canterbury untenable. Consequently, at the go-between Templar's House at Ewell Minnis, a little north-west of Dover, in the presence of the papal legate Pandulf on 15 May 1213, he was forced to accept Innocent III's decree to install Langton and to make good all the losses the church in England had suffered under his rapacity. John paid nine golden marks for this absolution – some say he borrowed it from the Templars. The legate formally made England and Ireland papal colonies: for an annual rent of 1,000 marks paid to Rome, John would be allowed to continue to reign by the Pope without opposition from other rulers. With John now a Vatican vassal the papal officials were quick to send into England a greatly increased number of their agents as 'enforcers' to ensure compliance with Rome's dictates, and to collect as much ready cash as possible to send back to the papal Crusades' coffers. This proliferation of 'foreign' papal controllers throughout the land on an innocent English public was to virtually entrap Hubert at a future time.[1]

The Channel coast opposite England being now under the rule of the French meant that all British shipping to the English possessions had to run south-west around the Brest peninsula across Biscay to La Rochelle. To this end John had Hubert working out of La Rochelle co-ordinating troop and supplies movements in a kind of roll-on/roll-off operation, as well as at the same time overseeing the negotiation of trade agreements between the Poitevin barons and merchants. The Templars order also had their private wharves at La Rochelle, which Hubert was also expected to protect. The hinterland of La Rochelle, with its capital at Niort, was the leading Atlantic coast trading region; but dominating its general cargo business were two commodities which provided vast revenues all year round – wine and salt.

The incomparable Bordeaux vineyards shipped their products to thirsty customers across all Europe and, as well, north to the Scandinavian and Hanseatic states. Vineyards had existed in England since the Romans, but by Hubert's time were largely grown under monastic viticulture husbandry – with questionable vintages. One English viveur comparing the English grapes with those of Bordeaux said the former could only be imbibed through clenched teeth, with closed eyes! It is very likely that during his time there Hubert was involved in the annual 'Tamwyn' shipping delivery to Queenhithe in London. A small fleet of ships especially modified to carry the 'tonneau' sized barrels (900l each) set sail each year bound for London's Queenhithe dock – the fleet was called the 'Tamwyn', being wine for delivery to the Thames. On arrival in the Thames Estuary the mercantile role of the ships was exchanged for one of a form of regatta. Firstly, all the vessels had to congregate at a point down-river off Yantlet Creek, where a vessel to lead the convoy was chosen; then, in line-astern of the vanguard ship (always identified as the 'Tamwyn'), the fleet processed up to Queenhithe dressed overall in bunting and flags, to the accompaniment of their crews singing their Kyrie Eleison. Having arrived at Queenhithe they were not allowed to dock and unload for two ebb and one high tide. (To dry out?) The subsequent scenes on Queenhithe dockside can be imagined. Today, just behind the Queenhithe dock, the hall of the Vintners guild (dating from the eleventh century) still stands. The parish church of St Michael Queenhythe also stood nearby. After its demolition in 1867 its unique weathervane of a medieval ship was refitted atop St Nicholas Cole Abbey, where it can be seen today. Hubert would have worked with countless ships like that one. Yantlet Creek, on the Isle of Grain, marked the limit of the City of London's Thames jurisdiction in those days. The other La Rochelle commodity, and which Hubert would have controlled, was the ever available salt – vital and valuable to all countries. La Rochelle's 'Bay Salt' was harvested in the local waters in huge tonnages and exported across Europe and to Middle Eastern countries, principally for food preservation. It was a perennial high income earner for the La Rochelle locality.

As mentioned, a further fleet based at La Rochelle over which Hubert had control was that belonging to the Knights Templar. With licences to land in Rye, Winchelsea and Portsmouth the Templar Atlantic fleet ships were kept busy all year round sailing between La Rochelle and the south coast ports. They also unshipped at Dover their own grocery and drink supplies from the English-controlled Gascony province. The Templar Middle East fleet was based at Marseilles, and this too sent ships back and forth to La Rochelle. This multitude of ships sailing across the Channel and between Mediterranean ports carried, apart from all manner of material and foodstuffs, men, horses and pilgrims, all in some way going to or returning from Holy Land destinations. The vast numbers of horses sailed in specially adapted galleys called 'busses'. These had adapted sterns with drop-down ramps for the horses to access the hold. An average 'buss' held forty horses and riders, plus the sailing crew. Hubert of course had to manage the port stabling of these numerous horses as they awaited onward transit to other lands, and not to mention all kinds of farm animals as well. He must have had several hundred dock workers, manual and clerical, working under his deputy managers, twenty-four hours each day, throughout the year. With these wide-ranging maritime activities under his personal control, not surprisingly Hubert became a very competent port manager and, by association, also accumulated a sophisticated knowledge of ship handling and fleet movements in the waters of the Channel and the Mediterranean. It was a skill that he was to bring to the saving of England in times to come. Doubtless too Hubert also looked to his own creature comforts through a reliable supply of *ex officio* 'presents' finding their way to his offices, in Niort and London. It is quite possible too that Hubert, with his linguistic skills, took time to learn the basics of that region's patois – the old Occitan tongue in which the natives would communicate between themselves.

Although the continental Channel coast had become a no-go area for the English, the Channel itself certainly wasn't. The excommunicate John had already had one attempt at forestalling a papally approved French invasion when on 30 May 1213 he sent a contingent of his new navy under the command of his half-brother William Longsword, Earl of Salisbury, to attack the French fleet at anchor at the port of Damme, upstream from Bruges. To John's credit the foray was successful and Philip's fleet and invasion plans wrecked. John's emergent Royal Navy then found its sea legs with a programme of continual harrying of any suspicious craft found in the

Channel waters; the French – and vessels under the command of Eustace the Monk – coming in for special attention.

John disembarked at La Rochelle on 15 February 1214 with his expeditionary army aimed at recovering some of his inheritance overrun by the de Lusignan knights. (Previously he had done a deal with a Templars' shipyard in Spain to buy himself his own special vessel for £133 for the journey – it was insured through the London Templars' office.) Accompanied by Hubert, John immediately started his attack on this powerful family headed by brothers Hugh and Geoffrey opposing English control of Poitou. After John's besieging of their castles at Mervant and Vouvant, Geoffrey capitulated and on 25 May, at Parenay, signed a peace treaty, witnessed by Hubert de Burgh. John then moved north of the Loire taking Ancenis, Nantes, Beaufort and Angers in quick succession. Hubert now parted company with the King as John ordered him to stay and hold Angers, the Angevin capital, while the main English army continued its expedition. But although these towns fell to John's forces, they were only towns, not militarily significant obstacles; John had not attempted to attack any of the great fortresses the control of which was essential to any successful outcome of his hopes of territorial reclamation.

Finally, on 27 July 1214 John's cobbled-together coalition expeditionary force at Bouvines Bridge came face to face in a showdown with King Philip II heading a vast army recruited mostly from the surrounding communes, all with close family ties and bound together by the common purpose of destroying John's invading conglomerate mercenaries. According to one authority describing the French army,

> There is not a single knight, sergeant, or foot soldier from south of the Loire: that area is another world. The royal army at Bouvines is primarily that of old Francia: in fact it is the Frankish army.[2]

In contrast John headed a force formed from a shaky alliance of forces under John's nephew, King Otto of Germany; the Earl of Salisbury, William Longsword; Ferrand, Count of Flanders; and lastly Renaud Dammartin, Count of Boulogne. All were on promises of great things – if they were on the winning side. A modern historian has detailed the flow of the Battle of Bouvines Bridge, literally blow by blow,[3] taking for her source the saga written by William the Breton who claimed to be at the battle. Translated from his saga-speak by Andree Duby, William's detail of medieval hand-to-hand fighting to the death is certainly chillingly real, so at this point a short digression is taken to further understand from William's saga the features of medieval weaponry and its use in battle as it was in Hubert's time, as Hubert wore it and wielded it, and, as well, what protective measures, if any, could be taken against it. William's words are medieval on-the-spot reporting at its best. Firstly, he sets the scene …

He makes the opening point that defence spending has been supporting the breeding of heavy battle horses, also the development growth of the iron metallurgy industry for weapons manufacture. But he sees it 'unfair' that weapons are being devised to remove any honour concept from the battlefield. Forged steel hooks on staves are used to unhorse armoured knights. Or, as William sees it, they are 'weapons of the mercenary, they disregard honour, they turn the rules of the game around. Those hooks destroy the social order. With them soldiers of low birth bring down from their mounts men of the highest ranks, they harpoon them by the edges of their armour – the hooks are the image of subversion itself. And then, thin well-sharpened knives can penetrate the joints of the unhorsed knight's armour, reach up to the tenderness of the flesh and pierce it.' Updated protective measures he describes as: 'To the hauberk, the long split tunic woven out of fine iron mail, they now know how to add metal sleeves and chausses which cover the arms all the way to below the wrists, and the legs down to the ankles. The hauberk now extends toward the neck through a protective cover of the nape of the neck and the chin, which they called a *ventaille*, and which itself gradually tends to disappear under a helmet extending towards the lower part of the face and taking the shape of a full cylinder with only a few narrow openings for seeing and breathing. Thus the interstices through which death can enter have been reduced. The would-be killer must now aim carefully at the eye-holes or dig towards the hollows of the groin through the narrow apertures left between the chausses and the hauberk to allow horsemen to relieve themselves. Killing thus requires a skilful cracking of the right assemblage, in other words, it has become an art.' This is an epoch when, even though the monetary income of knights is continually growing, they have to struggle to provide their sons with the best available fighting equipment. It is primarily the high cost of weapons that makes for the chequered look of the mass of fighters on the field of Bouvines. To begin with, there are the foot-soldiers who are from the class of the poor, most having been conscripted in the communes by order of the prince. They are the unlucky ones, the rotten apples, the misfits, or perhaps those slower to hide than others. Their neighbours have betrayed them. Equipped with odds and ends, with only leggings, a leather tunic, at best an iron hat, to protect their bodies, they are the ones who are going to die. As for the horsemen, noble or not, many still wear the old pointed helmet with the large nose guard of the Bayeux Tapestry and, as best they can, take refuge behind their shields against low blows to their limbs and stomach. Only the rich are well-protected. The skin of those princes who have gone so far as to armour their horses cannot be seen, which for all intents and purposes renders them unrecognizable. Hence, the importance of rallying signs: the cries, the banners held up next to each captain, the heraldic symbols sewn on the 'coats of arms' which are types of surplices of light material that flap over the armour but which tear quickly, soon turning to tatters, and whose ruin makes strangers out of those wearing them. Mistaken identities are a common occurrence, thus each and everyone is forced to scream out his name through the holes in his helmet. Every fray is a tornado of emblems, a din of calls and invectives, and, in the wheat's trampled dust, a whirlpool of tangled signs. William then gets into the Battle of Bouvines proper. 'Gautier of Ghistelle and Buridan, who were knights of noble prowess, were exhorting the knights of their echelon to battle. They were then met by the battalion of Champenois, and they attacked and fought each other valorously. When their lances broke, they pulled out their swords and exchanged wondrous blows. Into this fray appeared Peter of Rémy and the men of his company; by force they captured and brought away this Gautier of Ghistelle and John Buridan. But a knight of their group called Eustache of Malenghin began to yell out loud with great arrogance "Death, death to the French!" and the French began to surround him. One stopped him and took hold of his head between his arm and his chest, and then ripped his helmet off his head, while another struck him to his heart with a knife between the chin and the *ventaille* and made him feel through great pain the death with which he had threatened the French through great arrogance. Also Michael of Harmes was hit with a lance between the hauberk and the thigh. He was pinned to his saddlebow and horse, and both he and the horse were thrown to the ground!' For this account suffice to say that when things started getting hot, Otto opted out and fled from the field and the domino effect that then ensued resulted in the wholesale rout of the English army. The English leaders Longsword, Dammartin, and Ferrand and many other lesser magnates were captured for eventual ransom. The disaster was enough for the Poitevin barons in John's army, they turned tail and went home, leaving John now heavily outnumbered against the oncoming French. (Andree Duby's translation continues on for many pages of detail describing the infighting for any reader wishing to experience medieval sword, lance and axe handling in life or death battles as seen from the inside.)

But an expected final *coup de grâce* by Philip didn't happen; the Pope had decided to intervene. Supervised by Cardinal Robert Curzon a two-week truce commencing 30 August was implemented, and the English envoys headed by Hubert (whom John had delegated) met the French delegation at the convent of Fuleirelle, near Chinon, to sign an agreement that John could retain only the Angevin lands south of the Loire. The Battle of Bouvines Bridge marked the start of the permanent English retreat from the European continent; everywhere to the north of the Loire was now lost to John for good – and he had it in writing. Also agreed at this meeting was that the truce between Philip and John was to last for five years from September 1214. A curious sidelight to this peace treaty signing was a display of personal animosity towards Hubert by one of the commissioners, Earl Ranulph of Chester, who felt Hubert was of insufficient authority to authorize such a nationally important document. This stand-off between the hereditary belted earl and the seemingly johnny-come-lately streetwise Seneschal clearly had its roots in past times when John had humiliated Ranulph by reapportioning lands to Hubert in 1199 that the earl rightfully regarded as his family's inheritance. At Chinon Hubert signed himself as 'Hubert of Bourg, Seneschal of Poitou'.

The Anglo-French battle at Bouvines, 1214, falls into the same league as Hastings 1066 – neither country was ever the same again, nor did either country ever fully trust the other again. The 'them and us' Anglo/

French dichotomy, which has persisted to a greater or lesser degree down the centuries to modern times, was implanted and crystallized in both populations at Bouvines. Indeed, the formal claim of the English court to rights over the French monarchy only ceased with the Concordat of 1801. But, and of infinitely greater importance, is the fact that Bouvines opened the way in England for the genesis of Magna Charta – and that was going to change everything!

Chapter 7

1215 Rebellion and Magna Charta

W hen John crept back to England in October 1214 accompanied by a large force of mercenaries to take on the mounting baronial opposition to his rule, he left Hubert in Poitou to try and regain some semblance of administrative control over the residual Angevin continental domain. Hubert's success can be measured by the steady export of supplies and mercenary troop reinforcements that he kept up in response to John's constant appeals for more of everything during the winter of 1214–15. By the spring Hubert had tallied up a loan from the Knights Templars of some 1,100 marks to finance these operations. Meanwhile, John, to buttress his standing with Rome, sent in February an emissary to keep Pope Innocent III onside in his cause. He continued to egg his survival pudding with his vow in March to go on Crusade.

In John's absence much of the rebel leadership opposing the King emanated from the East Anglian region, notable leaders being Robert Fitzwalter and Eustace de Vesci. In fact East Anglian barons were to account for nearly half the twenty-five eventual signatories who proposed to enforce Magna Charta. It was in November 1214 that the fuse of rebel opposition to John's rule was lit, when a gathering of these leaders took place at Bury St Edmunds. According to chronicler Roger of Wendover, they intended to force John to recognize the terms of his coronation oath based on his predecessor's, Henry I, coronation charters. John's response (while playing for time) to these initial baronial demands was to defer any decision to a meeting of the Great Council on Epiphany, 6 January 1215. Unfortunately, a party of the barons hijacked the meeting by appearing threateningly in full armour and weaponry. This played right into John's hands and he immediately pronounced that he would not recognize their 'ancient and customary liberties' and additionally 'never accede to demands for such liberties from them or their successors'. Hubert received his recall orders in the May of 1215 and arrived back in England just after the rebel forces organized by Reginald de Cornhill (former Sheriff of Kent and Richard I's mariner builder) had on 17 May taken control of the City of London, the gates having been left open for them by the citizenry led by Lord Mayor William Hardell. John put Hubert in control of all the foreign forces with Philip d'Aubigny as his deputy and, on 24 May, in an attempt to disrupt communications with the rebel forces in the Home Counties, set siege to Rochester Castle, from where Reginald de Cornhill was directing the rebellion against John. Although a truce at Rochester was agreed a week or so later, the rebel barons had gained the initiative in the national administration; also, to address their grievances under John's rule, they had compiled the first draft of Magna Charta – 'The Articles of the Barons'. On 15 June 1215, almost the complete baronage of England, both in support of and in opposition to John, met with the King at Runnymede near Windsor to try and reach a settlement of their differences. Runnymede was chosen being midway between the barons' headquarters at Staines, and John's Windsor Castle. After three days of horse-trading, threat, bluff and counter-bluff by the participants, John with great reluctance (and no intention of commitment) on 19 June put his seal to the first crude version of this unique treaty between a King and the people he ruled. In its first draft form Magna Charta comprised 49 'Articles of the Barons'; however by the date of its ratification on 19 June this had been expanded to 63 articles to include also a revision of the laws relating to the great forested areas of the realm which at that time were substantial, widespread and the source of considerable profit to those living in and around them. More and more John and his largely foreign administration had illegally encroached upon these natural resources.[1] Additionally, articles 40 and 41 required John to 'remove completely from office' a list of named Angevin favourites and, as well, '… foreign knights, mercenaries, cross-bowmen, routiers and serjeants, who come with horses and arms to the detriment of this kingdom'.[2]

Although *ex officio* supportive of John, the forceful Hubert can be imagined, keeping his options open, standing at the King's shoulder, but at the same time while heeding closely the barons' arguments, being careful not to exhibit too overt a dissent to either royal or baronial cause. Adding their names to the original draft were 25 of the rebel barons who undertook to make the King adhere to the charter terms, though how they envisaged doing this is not clear. John countered their invigilation upon him by listing 38 of his own court to oversee the actions of the rebels' 25. Hubert was the senior signatory of the 38 and, as such, maybe too he was a principal instigator of this idea? In any event, Hubert would have known that he was at Runnymede as a main player in an historical event the like of which he would never again experience. On that day, he must have felt the tangible weight of an expectant national population's hopes beginning to bear down. By virtue of his long standing as John's right-hand man, Hubert certainly played a dominant part as one of the arbitrators between the barony and the King. Indeed the Magna Charta text affirms Hubert, amongst other signatories, advising John to affix his seal to the document. How much the final draft of the 1215 Charter owes to Hubert's efforts cannot now be known; it is certain that his authoritative voice would have been prominent (conjointly with that of his ally and confidant, Archbishop of Canterbury, Stephen Langton) not least because his own well-being was tied to the document having to work in the future. In fact Hubert would, in that future, adduce to his own defence to save his life, the momentous terms of Chapter 39 of the Great Charter of 1215:

> No free man shall be taken or imprisoned or dispossessed or outlawed or exiled or in any way ruined, nor will we [the King] go or send against him, except by the lawful judgements of his peers or by the law of the land.

Two original Magna Charta copies survive in the British Library while copies of the final 63 article version bearing Hubert's name are in the cathedrals of Lincoln and Salisbury.[3]

One contributor to a highly respected authority on Kent history records the fascinating possibility that Hubert returned to Dover from Runnymede with the original documents in his possession – 'the Articles' submitted by the Barons to John. These unique, and today priceless, parchments are supposed to have become, states the writer, buried among thousands of other official documents kept in safe custody within Dover Castle, and so were lost to contemporary knowledge. It is quite believable that Dover Castle in those times represented the nearest parallel to the modern safety deposit box (on a national scale) and, as such, the most secure place to store such important state documents, the fortress at the time being the most impregnable structure in the land.[4] However, a more modern account[5] relates that one of the present copies in the British Library had, in 1215, been taken to the Cinque Ports and was later discovered at Dover Castle in 1630 and acquired from the then Constable by the collector and antiquarian, Sir Robert Cotton. Then, by a most circuitous and hazardous route over the subsequent decades, it came to rest in the British Museum on the latter's acquisition of the Cottonian MSS collection in 1753. If the tradition is true, then this Magna Charta copy (which Hubert may have taken back to Dover after Runnymede in 1215) can be seen today at the British Library as Cotton Charter XIII 31a. A copy of the 'Articles of the Barons' also exists today, in the British Library, as Additional MSS 4938. It survived, after a long incarceration in the archives of Lambeth Palace, to eventually emerge from the possessions of the Earl of Stanhope who, in 1769, presented it to the nation. An interesting sidelight to the 1215 Magna Charta is that it appears John also updated his charter to the Channel Islands. He is said to have absented himself from England to visit them and confirm in person the charter known as 'The Constitutions of King John'. Its medieval provisions served the islands (problematically) until 1860 when a Royal Commission debated their applicability to modern times. It found the Charter to still be authentic and some of its original provisions still survive in law.

By now Hubert had become again a power at John's side to be reckoned with – a remarkable achievement considering barely a decade had elapsed since Chinon when he had been vilified by John as the villain of the piece; also for more than half this decade Hubert had been absent abroad from the Court. Clearly he had come to know the ins and outs of the Angevin administration, both at home and abroad, better than most others at court, perhaps even better than John: he had learned how to 'work the system'. And, vitally, he had his own wide following of English friends and advisors at court to keep him updated on any event of significance – he was perhaps John's best informed courtier. Hubert's actions at this period display a towering personality, a commanding presence, and a consummate ability in power politics at the highest level that even John was forced to recognize. This recognition took tangible form when, towards the end of the Runnymede conference, John held a ceremony at which '... in the presence of Lord Stephen, archbishop of Canterbury, the earl of Warenne, the earl of Ferrars and other magnates he conferred on Hubert de Burgh the role of Chief Justiciar of England.'[6]

In medieval courts the Justiciar was a post of vice-regality: if the King left England, authority to oversee national affairs would automatically devolve upon the Justiciar. It is likely that the influence of Hubert's East Anglian neighbour, the great Earl of Warenne, was a factor in Hubert's appointment forcing as it did the resignation of the existing Poitevin Justiciar, Peter des Roches, Bishop of Winchester. He had been a prominent cause of the civil unrest by his arbitrary imposition of John's manic demands upon the country's working population; but though des Roches had to concede his position now to appease the barons, Hubert was to feel the vicious backlash of this disaffected courtier in future times.

Chapter 8

Henry III, 1216 and After

1215–1217 Civil War and Invasion

The events at Runnymede settled little: the rebellious barony had dictated to John its requirements for a better management of the kingdom; John had grudgingly conceded there may be a case to answer on some points. In fact the 1215 Charter was nowhere near being a manageable definitive document; but more a work in progress wish list. Much of its still raw terms of reference remained contentious to both peers and population: while these issues awaited their final settlement, the country was taking to arms – for and against John. Both parties considered that any changes would be wrought more with hostile weaponry than with parchment and quill. A further catalyst which stoked up the flames of rebellion was the issue of a papal bull on 24 August 1215 in response to John's request to annul the Charter.[1] Pope Innocent III had acceded to John's request to intervene as the kingdom continued to be a vassal of the papal see while John ruled, and so the barons could not enforce any amendments to John's regal status without the prior agreement of Rome. This was not to be forthcoming and John, now backed by the Vatican, played his 'get out of jail' card for all it was worth. Hubert knew his position now as Justiciar automatically made him a principal leader of the Royalist party in their forthcoming war with the opposing barony which comprised both English and Angevin interests. It was a responsibility Hubert would never abandon.

After June 1215 the baronial rebels returned to London to strengthen their enforced occupation of the capital, at the same time John continued to amass his largely mercenary force to support those Royalist lords still adherent to his cause. With most of south-east England still in rebel control, by September it was unsafe for John to travel by road so, in company with Hubert, he set out from Portsmouth to Dover by boat with the intention of keeping his court at Dover. It was not his newly acquired authority as Chief

Justice that Hubert intended to exercise in taking this journey, because all the court and legal chambers at Westminster were held by the rebels, rather he was on his way to reassume the castellanship of Dover Castle. On 25 June, before leaving Runnymede, he had been confirmed in this prestigious post by John, and to augment his control of the Home Counties he was appointed Sheriff of Surrey, Kent, Norfolk and Suffolk. The impending civil war was to continually involve these East Anglian honours of Hubert, but his personal role was to be played out in Dover Castle, which he himself described as 'the key to England'.[2]

From August 1215 the rebel forces skirmished back and forth across Kent while John was there, resulting in Rochester Castle being again laid under siege by his Royalists. After his failure to take the fortress John sent for Hubert to come up from Dover and help. Hubert arrived with a contingent of his men, assessed the situation at the massive square-towered Norman fort, and decided that mining a corner tower foundation was the best option. Having dug out a vast cavity under the south-west tower and propped the super-incumbent masonry with tree trunks, Hubert then purchased '40 fat bacon pigs, the least good for eating' and, using this mountain of inflammable grease, fired the props and collapsed the tower. The rebels, with a fatally damaged castle and no resources left, surrendered a month later on 30 November. Feeling better for his Justiciar's practical lesson in castle demolition, John left Hubert to return to Dover while he marched north with his mercenaries to take on the rebel forces there. His illegitimate half-brother, William Longsword, Earl of Salisbury, meanwhile cut a swathe across the counties immediately north of the Thames, leaving the control and containment of Kent and Surrey to Hubert operating out of Dover Castle. At Dover, Hubert spent long hours on the castle battlements (doubtless fingering the decades of his Rosary) looking across the Channel for any hint of the invasion that the rebel forces had tried to coerce Louis, the King of France's heir, into attempting. The French father and son had taken the precaution of presenting their case for attacking John to the Pope and the consequent time delay allowed Hubert the chance to spend the time not only making Dover Castle impregnable, but also increasing the security of the whole Kent coastline, ensuring too he had good communications through the densely forested Weald out to the Royalist strongholds.

Wherever Hubert was in command of a fortification he was always to exhibit an innate skill in quickly getting to know the lie of the surrounding land, and also the people with the local knowledge most likely to be beneficial to his efforts. In this respect at Dover he had been liaising with a Kentish leader called William of Cassingham. Most likely of Flemish origin, William (the French were to call him 'Willikin of the Weald') lived near Kensham (hence 'Cassingham') by Rolvenden, and was the leader of a band of woodland brigands-cum-poachers who knew every hide and hollow way through the almost impenetrable forests that then covered most of what is today East Sussex and West Kent, and which stretched south from the North Downs to the borders of Romney Marsh. Very much in the way that, in later centuries, their smuggling descendants in the same locality would operate through a sophisticated web of parish informants, so the followers of William (who numbered thousands) controlled the lines of communication between London, North Kent, and the vitally important Cinque Ports coast where it was expected any French invasion force would attempt to land. From his Rolvenden centre of operations it was relatively simple for William to assemble his irregulars at any chosen point very quickly, either by use of their intimate knowledge of the cross-country lanes networking through the forests, or by boat along the nearby River Rother at Smallhythe. The Rother met the Channel at Rye barely four miles away and inland, at Smallhythe, formed a deep, navigable waterway with an active shipbuilding industry.[3] An uncompromising antagonist in defence of his adopted homeland, William would live to see his guerrilla operations rewarded by his monarch.[4] He exemplified the assertion of that lover of Sussex rural life, Rudyard Kipling, that,

> a hard-bitten, South-country poacher makes the best man-at-arms you can find.'[5]

But despite all these precautions an advance guard of the French invasion force – a 'special forces' unit if you like – had successfully landed in the Thames Estuary that December and joined up with the rebel force in the capital to prepare the ground for the main army to follow. They did not have long to wait.

To counter the impending invasion, by May 1216 all the transports and fighting galleys that could be sheltered there had been amassed in the Cinque Ports harbours. But the shelter was to prove insufficient against the vagaries of the English weather and a hurricane-force storm through the night of 18/19 May capsized much of the fleet at its moorings. Also watching and waiting across the Channel, Louis was quick to hear about the destruction of the greater part of the English ships and, with the confirmation of the inability of a British sea force to oppose him, accepted the rebel barons' offer and set sail to invade. With a sense of greater impending disaster than that which had prevailed in 1066, John, Peter des Roches and the now ragtag Royalist military fled to Winchester. Many of John's mercenaries now perceived Louis as a more promising paymaster and defected from the Royalist cause to await the arrival of the invaders. Once again Hubert de Burgh was left surrounded by an all-powerful French force and with an English king disappearing over the horizon. But there was one crucial difference now – Hubert was on his home ground, at the same time he knew that one false move in his defensive strategy for Dover could well lead to the loss of the English crown to Louis. In his mind the possibility was distant, but not improbable, that England for the first time in its history was in danger of becoming part of the French kingdom. It was Chinon all over again: but this time with the crown of England going to the winner!

Louis' invasion force, comprising some 1,200 knights with many thousand followers, landed on the Kent coast near Stonor unopposed between 20–24 May 1216. During the next week he ignored Dover but instead set out straight for London where he knew a friendly reception awaited. Taking the castles at Canterbury and Rochester en route, he arrived on 2 June at the gates of the capital which the rebel force had opened to him. From London, with his force now swelled by the disaffected English barons, including the Earls of Arundel, Salisbury, Aumale and their followers, Louis next set out to capture the strategic castles of the south and east. Winchester quickly fell next, following which, during July, his army moved north to rampage over much of central England and in so doing, kept those forces adherent to John penned up against the Welsh border. It was a terrifying ordeal for the rural English citizenry for, as the annalist of Waverley recorded: 'these barbarous aliens and other wicked plundered from the Kingdom of France, set villages alight, did not spare churches or cemeteries, took and despoiled all kinds of men by harsh and hither-to unheard-of bodily tortures ...!'

They also had to live off the land and from the surviving Pipe Rolls of the autumn of 1216 we can read that at Bishop's Waltham Manor a French raiding party led by Geoffrey de Lucy made off with 54 quarters of grain, 53 of oats, 8 plough horses, 12 oxen, 408 ewes, and 199 hogs. They were guarded but were hopelessly outnumbered. In like manner the King's routine collection of rents and other income dues from the manorial estates was made up as it went along. Quick to fill the vacuum of safe depositories was the Order of the Knights Templar who made available their large and sophisticated safe custody facilities in the west at Portsmouth and Bristol. From these 'banks' the Templars found ways to keep up a steady flow of ready cash to the Royalist forces. Louis (and as his father Philip had strongly advised against) continued to bypass the two most significant castles, Windsor and Dover, reserving them for special treatment at a future time. From the north the Scots king, Alexander, took Carlisle and headed south to offer allegiance to Louis; his northern realm had been as badly disaffected by John as had been England. Not every castle fell to Louis; some Royalist fortresses (e.g. Lincoln and Norwich) held out but became isolated as the invasion swept past to invest the lands around these strongholds. Where this happened Louis left a small force to stay and lay siege to prevent the occupants receiving outside help. It was a policy that was to progressively fragment and deplete the men available to his invasion effort. Lesser castles such as Reigate, Guildford, and even Peter Des Roches' Farnham Castle, were also quickly overrun during June and July. But taking these lesser castles had unforeseen consequences: they were mostly only manned by token forces. At Odiham castle for instance, after a two-week siege by Louis' men, the French were galled to discover that the defending force amounted to only three knights and ten sergeants!

About 25 July Louis sent an assault force commanded by the Counts of Nevers and Dreux to take Windsor Castle; meanwhile he led his army down to Dover to take on Hubert de Burgh. Louis had probably been less than well informed of the task ahead as he stood at a safe distance looking up at the castle's independently defensive barbican, walls, baileys, and the deep, steep moat surrounding the massive keep itself. In prior years both

Richard the Lionheart, John himself, and their father Henry II before them had added to and improved this '*Clavis Angliae*', 'key to England', as Louis' father had reminded him. Now, additional to all these previous efforts, Hubert de Burgh had completed his own refinements over the past months: Dover had been rendered as impregnable as was possible within the military technological limits of the age. Inside the castle awaiting the French onslaught was Hubert's hand-picked force led by some 150 knights and Flemish mercenaries upon whose allegiance he could count augmenting these was his primary defensive measure – a large contingent of the best crossbowmen he could recruit, and Hubert was skilled at acquiring quality, in whatever field. Determined to pile on the difficulty and unnerve the French, Hubert took pre-siege opportunities to parade his force, armed and armoured, outside the Barbican main gate, leaving Louis with no illusions about what awaited him. The best authority on the Dover siege by someone who was there is the *Histoire des Ducs de Normandie at des Rois d'Angleterre*, and this anonymous witness reports that on one occasion when Hubert's men were outside the castle gate a French crossbowman named Ernaut chanced his arm to take a close shot: he missed, but Hubert's men didn't and frogmarched the hapless Ernaut back into the castle.

In mid-July Louis had made up his mind and set his siege in motion. Half his force he left in occupation of Dover town, the remainder set up camp outside the castle. At the same time he sent some of his ships out into the Channel to cut off any attempt to reinforce the castle via the coast.

His stone-throwers – mangonels and perriers – now started to pound the main gate with huge rocks, while siege towers were erected against the north walls. While these measures were in force the French mining teams started to tunnel under Hubert's timber *enceinte* (encircling wall) to get to the Barbican. A small breach was the result of their efforts, but on trying to exploit this opening the French found themselves exposed in a killing field when they attempted to cross the open ground to the Outer Bailey, and even then the Inner Ward and then the Keep awaited their efforts. With his forces suffering hundreds of casualties from continuous volleys of Hubert's crossbowmen firing their lethally flighted bolts down from dozens of well-protected enfilade apertures, Louis was forced to retire his stone-throwers to a safe distance and rethink his options. While so doing his force was increased by the contingent he had sent to Windsor to take the castle there. Having after two months found Windsor too difficult a nut to crack with the limited resources at their disposal, these mercenaries had reasoned there would be better pickings back at Dover with the main force.

It was mid-August and Louis had brought up further heavy artillery in the form of a Malveisine catapult to try and create a more damaging breach in the mostly heavy wooden Dover outer barbican, this would allow a frontal assault on the massive Outer Bailey wall. The Malveisine was successful, and the bravest of the French were led through the enlarged breach by the standard-bearer of Bethune, Huart de Paon – and that was as far as they got, the towering masonry of the Outer Bailey (17–21ft thick walls) offering an altogether more intimidating challenge. The standard-bearer was killed. It was not until mid-September that Louis' mining engineers, working under withering fire from Hubert's crossbowmen, created a fall of masonry under one of the main gates into the Outer Bailey and effected a small opening. This was quickly closed up with massive timbers by the defenders and several of Louis' leading knights were killed in continuing the attempted assault, including Philip's brother-in-law, Guichard de Beaujeau. The French retreated back to the Barbican but then had to vacate this as Hubert moved his defensive archers forward after them into better positions to pick off the invaders.

Louis decided not to pursue a further frontal attack and instead surrounded the castle with a large siege 'village' of his forces to try and starve Hubert's force out. By mid-October this ploy still had not succeeded and many French knights, discomfited by the arduous demands of a long and unrelenting campaign which was showing virtually no reward for their efforts, and was now being made even more miserable by the onset of the English autumn rains, just packed up their rusting armour and took the next boat home to the sunny peace of their vineyards. Assessing this situation, Hubert felt he could tempt Louis to agree to a short truce. In medieval siege situations truce agreements were part and parcel of the conflict, rather like a half-time interval, with both sides bound by an unwritten chivalric law to observe the truce's verbally agreed terms. So on 14 October a brief cessation was agreed to allow Hubert to confer with John what should happen next. What did happen next was that John died! In Newark Castle, during the night of 17–18 October, the recalcitrant monarch breathed his last aged 49, having lost the majority of his inherited continental dominions, the trust of much of his kingdom, not to mention his personal treasure in the Wash through misreading the tides. Hubert headed back to Dover Castle, mindful that he was now in a new world.

Chapter 9

24 August 1217 The Great Battle of Sandwich: Hubert's Finest Hour

John's son Henry from his marriage to Isabella of Angouleme was aged only 9 at the death of his father; he would be unable to rule in his own name until he came of age nearly a decade hence. At the time of his father's death the prince and his mother were sheltering in Corfe Castle. There were no precedents for the political situation that now existed: a minor acceding to the crown at the same time as an invading foreign contender for that same crown was running riot across the country. Louis therefore now sought to act before the Royalists could reorganize themselves. He took the initiative by sending John's illegitimate half-brother, William Longsword, Earl of Salisbury, down to Dover to confront Hubert and demand the surrender of the castle, there being now no monarch of an age to rule for whom to defend it.

This was without doubt the most seminal moment in the siege of Dover Castle: the annalist Matthew Paris thought so too and, having gathered all the details of the scenario that was played out on the day, wrote up the following account which is unique in English history.

Louis, thinking to corrupt the fidelity and fineness of Hubert de Burgh, by trying his avarice, sent word that he wished to have a peaceable talk with him; and when Hubert consented to this, Louis sent special messengers to him to a postern gate suitable for the talk. The messengers were the earl of Salisbury, William Longespee, who brought with him as a hostage Thomas de Burgh, brother of the said Hubert, who had been made prisoner by Louis at the castle of Norwich, and three of the most noble of the French. Hubert then came to the postern, followed by five cross-bow men with bows bent and arrows fitted, so that if there was necessity, they should not spare their enemies. Earl William then said 'The death of king John, once our lord, is no secret to you, Hubert, nor are you ignorant of the oath of Louis, who has sworn, that when he takes possession of this castle by force of arms, all found in it shall be hung without fail. Consult therefore your own safety and honour. You cannot long retain this castle; the power of our lord Louis increases daily, while that of the king decreases, by strong daily assaults; or you will at least perish of hunger, unless you be wise and yield to my advice, for you see all hope of help has vanished; therefore without any delay or difficulty, give up this castle to Louis, and you will not be branded with perfidy, since you cannot hold possession of it much longer.' Thomas, his brother, moreover said to Hubert with tears, 'My dear brother, have compassion on yourself, on me, and all of us, by yielding to the advice of these nobles; for we shall then all be freed from impending destruction.' Then the earl said 'Listen to my advice, Hubert, and obey the will of our lord Louis and he will give you, as an inheritance, the counties of Norfolk and Suffolk, and you will also become his chief counsellor and friend; but if you do not do this, your brother Thomas will be hung, and you in a short time will suffer the same punishment.' To this Hubert then replied 'Earl, wicked traitor that you are, although king John, our lord and your brother, be dead, he has heirs, your nephew, whom, although everybody else deserted him, you, his uncle, ought not to abandon, but ought to be a second father to him; why then, degenerate and wicked man that you are, do you dare talk thus to me? Let not Louis hope that I will surrender as long as I draw breath. Never will I yield to French aliens this Castle, which is the very key and gate of England!' Then, in a harsher tone, with a scowling look on him, Hubert added 'Do not speak another word, because by the lance of God, if you open your mouth to say anything more, you shall all be pierced with numbers of arrows, nor will I even spare my own brother!' The earl therefore, and those who were with him seeing that they would be killed in the flash of an eye, because the cross-bow men were ready to discharge their weapons, retreated at once, glad to escape alive and uninjured. When Louis heard this, although he was sorry and enraged, he greatly applauded the firmness of Hubert.

In this remarkable confrontation we can see the true Hubert in his full colours, taking on the enemy head-on with full confidence he will win – as devastating with the word as with the sword. His national rallying cry, 'Never will I yield …!' echoes down the centuries to take the form in recent times as 'We will never surrender!' All who were there that day would remember that Anglo/French face-off all their lives.

There was to be no compromise. Louis, defeated in word if not in fact, extended his truce with Hubert until February 1217 then turned his back on Dover and left on 4 November 1216 with a view to tackling some castles of lesser status to regain some credibility before returning to try again to crack Hubert de Burgh. As soon as he had gone Hubert opened the castle gates to allow his forces to replenish their provisions with those abandoned by the French in their siege camp. To see them through the coming winter Hubert also looked after his men with a commandeered shipment of 82 tuns of wine from the Bordeaux vineyards where, as Seneschal of Poitou, he had made many useful friendships. It would have been suicidal to drink from any water source within the castle.

It was deemed essential by Stephen Langton, William Marshal and papal legate Gualo that the nation should immediately officially and publicly crown the young Henry III as the rightful heir to John. This would establish a fixed focal point of English national administration upon which could be constructed, step by step, the recovery of the realm from the invaders and a consequent return to law and order. The coronation of the young King consequently took place at Gloucester Cathedral on 28 October 1216. Shortly afterwards, on 11 November, a meeting was convened at Bristol by the most senior magnates of the realm to discuss ways and means of directing the new reign under the continuing French invasion. Principal attendees included William Marshal the senior soldier of the country, the papal legate Cardinal Gualo, Peter des Roches Bishop of Winchester, Ranulph Earl of Chester, and Hubert de Burgh – the latter previously absent from the coronation because he was besieged at Dover. Hubert used his local truce with Louis as a safe conduct pass to get across the country to what was the most significant meeting of the national government since 1066. The Council was assembled to authorize a revised version of the Great Charta. This was considered an essential first requirement now that the principal objector to the Magna

Charta's existence had ceased to be. Also some kind of basic fiscal framework had to be put in place to effectively refinance the nation following John's consistent debilitating raids on the Treasury. The presence of a foreign army currently on the loose across the country resulted in the Charta's chapters being cut from 61 to 42. As examples, clearly redundant were the references (ch. 61) to a baronial committee to oversee John's adherence to its terms. Likewise, the terms controlling 'foreign mercenaries' were omitted, as were the 'release of hostages' provisions. The most important addition, however, was the insertion of a new clause (ch. 42) whereby it was decreed that the whole text in its entirety would be revisited again for Council deliberation as and when a future peace had been established in the kingdom. This revised Bristol version was issued to the shires and sees in November 1216.

As John's appointed Justiciar Hubert now wielded a power second only to that of the King. There is no doubt his was the dominant voice in the decisions that were taken at Bristol to see the country through the present war and on into Henry's minority rule. Though the old earl complained vociferously that, approaching 70, he was too old for the role, Gualo succeeded in persuading William Marshal to assume the regency with the title 'governor of the king and kingdom' with, as his natural second-in-command, Hubert as Justiciar. The Poitevin Bishop of Winchester, Peter des Roches, was appointed tutor to the young King during his minority years, a role which made him subordinate to Hubert. This, together with his previously enforced loss of the office of Justiciar, compounded the deadly enmity with which the jealous Poitevin regarded Hubert. High priority was given to bring the still recalcitrant barony under control across the country: many were enjoying a new freedom in determining their versions of law and order in opposition to those pursued under John's rule. While not exactly an amnesty, the revised version of Magna Charta had been issued with Hubert as a principal draftee and signatory, to address the most contentious of the rebel's demands and try and remove the *raison d'être* for their opposition to the crown. It was hoped this would begin to undermine the French Dauphin's position with the former Royalists in his following.

Calling on his experience as a renowned castellan administrator, Hubert now came up with a potent idea to turn Louis' plans in attacking the lesser English castles as an instrument towards the Dauphin's own defeat. He proposed letting him take those minor castles, with agreed surrender by truce; Louis would then have to expend time and men in garrisoning these forts of relatively low strategic value. The English troops thus released under truce from each such castle could then be diverted to augment the garrisons of the Royalist's major national defence centres such as Dover, Windsor and Lincoln. During the winter of 1216/17 the plan worked like clockwork, Hubert being able to add to Dover those men released under truce arranged by him in East Anglia, namely from Norwich and Orford Castles. While in March 1217, when Louis was absent briefly in France to arrange reinforcements, the rebel troops holding Chichester, Portchester, Southampton, Farnham, Winchester and Marlborough Castles were all released under truce because no relief was forthcoming from their French commanders who elected to keep themselves safe behind the gates of London. Hubert utilized these men in the south-east defences. While things were relatively quiet Hubert also looked again to the creature comforts of his Dover garrison. With siege water being strictly avoided, literally 'like the plague', on 23 March he arranged with William Marshal to dispatch a further shipful of wine to Dover for Philip d'Aubigny, Sea Captain of the Cinque Ports. The wine merchants were ordered to accompany the wine, and then sent on from Dover to Winchester where Marshal would pay them.

On Louis' return in April 1217 he found his attempts to land at Dover repelled by the greatly enlarged force there; also his siege village had been destroyed by William of Cassingham's men who had also accounted for hundreds of French who had been unwise enough to stray into the south-eastern forests looking for provisions to see them through the winter. According to the chronicler Roger of Wendover, 'I saw eaten by dogs a hundred of the men of France whom the English slew between Winchester and Romsey!' Consequently Louis bypassed Dover, set Sandwich on fire, and after agreeing a truce with Hubert, went instead to the West Country where his depleted forces there found themselves only holding the impotent castles they had emptied by truce. Meanwhile a further French contingent which landed near Dover after Louis' departure, was set upon by William of Cassingham's men as they attempted to move west across Kent and join up with the main French force. The forest tracks between Dover and

Lewes ran red with the blood of decapitated Frenchmen. When told of these continuing guerrilla attacks, Louis considered his truce with Hubert now broken, and he backtracked to besiege Dover once more with the new catapults landed by his ships. This second siege started on 12 May: it was to no avail as Hubert's strengthened and replenished defenders once more littered the castle approaches with dead and dying Frenchmen. Also Hubert had used his authority to co-ordinate the Cinque Ports fleet which, under the captaincy of Philip d'Aubigny, was able to sail out and repel an attempt to reinforce Louis by sea. Of the forty ships sent over from Calais eight were captured. This victorious English flotilla then returned to successfully blockade Dover harbour against any further attempt by the French to land supplies. In retaliation the French mounted an attack on Hythe and Romney, but their inhabitants had long been gone.

During this confrontation the main English Royalist force led by William Marshal and Peter des Roches had been harrying the French invaders across the Midlands, and in May 1217 the two leaders arrived outside Lincoln Castle to enforce the expulsion of the French siege forces. But before giving some detail of the ensuing battle, a glance at the Royalist leaders will be useful. Both were better qualified for Dad's Army duty than for hand-to-hand fighting in the front-line: William Marshal was 70 and Peter des Roches 63, the latter Bishop of Winchester having exchanged cope for cuirass. William Marshal had spent most of his life as a freelance tournament competitor across Europe and had sworn allegiance to both the French King Philip and to John. In his present appointment as Regent he was taking arms to keep his young King on the throne, while des Roches had a similar responsibility as the appointed mentor to Prince Henry. Both were creaking in all joints but nevertheless had made their way at the head of a large Royalist force to help a lady – Dame Nicola de la Haye, castellan of Lincoln. In his senior military status as Earl of Pembroke, William had amassed a force of some 250 crossbowmen supported by about 400 knights, these all heading a considerable number of foot soldiers. On 19 May, from her battlement lookout, Dame Nicola could discern the Royalist forces arriving to the north-west of the city. The French siege commander, Thomas Count of Perche, could see them also but decided he had sufficient men to counter any advance which would have to be made uphill. But other of the French leaders thought it best to hedge their bets by achieving occupation of the castle and, as well, repelling the Royalist advance.

As the two forces joined in battle Marshal's force brushed aside the French ground force and then advanced in a pincer attack via both the Newport Arch and as well through the west gate. Once ensconced around the castle walls the crossbowmen were able to fire down into the trapped French soldiers below. Considerable carnage amongst the French ensued, their leader, the Count of Perche being among the fatalities. Those of the French military who could run away did so, in a terror-stricken horde down Lincoln High Street and out across the surrounding countryside. The senior French baronial knights were taken prisoner for ransom, probably some 300 in number, according to chronicler Roger of Wendover – and valiant matriarch Dame Nicola was happy to have her castle back again. The battle, for ever after called the 'Fair of Lincoln', would take its place among the decisive battles of the realm. When news of the hand-bagging of his forces at Lincoln by the redoubtable Dame Nicola aided by the old earl reached Louis, as few of the survivors did, he immediately raised his (3rd) siege of Dover and raced out of Kent to relative safety behind the walls of London. He had fatally divided his forces between Lincoln in the north and Dover in the south, and had paid a heavy price.

During these events Philip of France had found it politically safer to reaffirm his alliance with Rome than to continue supporting his son's fight for the English throne, thus Louis' plea for more reinforcements from across the Channel went unheeded by his father. Only his mother came to his aid, and through the summer of 1217 Blanche of Castile amassed around Calais a considerable seaborne reinforcement fleet. Opposed to this on the English south coast were the ships, mostly adapted transports, of the Cinque Ports and a few 'secret weapons' previously built by Richard the Lionheart, kept in good order by John, and now sailing south from safe northern ports to support Hubert's channel sailors. These ships, a rare exhibition of Angevin naval thinking, were the galleys with sails and oars and devoted only to offensive use against other craft. They were fitted with raised fighting decks, 'forecastles', from which archers could fire downwards at opposing vessels. Their heavily armoured bows were designed to be aimed at and to smash their way into the sides of other vessels: they had been used to great effect by Richard I in 1191 off Beirut. European shipping at this time was almost exclusively commercial, with few craft designed purely for a belligerent role at sea; so Richard and John's war galleys perhaps represent the beginnings of the offensive/defensive Royal Navy. Hubert, in his role as Constable of the Cinque Ports mariners, assigned to Philip d'Aubigny, his deputy, the task of collecting, arming, and provisioning the motley collection of shipping now arriving by the hour at the Kent and Sussex Cinque ports. The entire thrust of Louis' plan for the crown of England was about to be crystallized into a short stretch of sea soon to be peopled by the final players in the drama. To back up Hubert at Dover, William Marshal had brought together most of the remaining Royalist infantry forces and spread them across the hinterland of Dover and Sandwich.

At Sandwich that fateful morning, 24 August 1217, on a day that was 'fine and clear and they could look far out at sea' – it was the Feast of St Bartholomew – most of the English fleet of assorted Cinque Ports and other craft assembled under Captain Philip d'Aubigny was ready to sail.[1]

It had been difficult for Hubert to assemble a combatant seaborne force anywhere the size needed to oppose the one now rapidly approaching. His biographer Matthew Paris records, 'There were given to his command about sixteen ships well fitted out, besides attendant small boats to the number of twenty.' Another chronicler, Roger of Wendover, gives a total not exceeding 'forty of galleys and other ships and fishing boats'. But Hubert's most significant vessels were a number of 'Cogs' – large ships, standing high out of the water, with 'castles' built fore and aft. They were manned by the most skilled men-at-arms who could aim downwards from them onto the enemy's decks. Accompanying this fleet was also a number of the iron-prowed galleys: after ramming a ship the oarsmen became an armed boarding party.

Hubert now left the safety of Dover Castle, having made his confession to Luke, his lifelong chaplain, and then in his own 'fine ship' led the rest of the fleet up the coast to assume command overall. Some of his principal fleet commanders under Philip d'Aubigny, were his uncle, Henry de Trubleville, Richard Seward from the Dover garrison, Richard Fitzjohn, nephew of the Earl of Warenne, and Sir Robert de Nerford, another of Hubert's relations from Norfolk. Meanwhile, at a safe distance from London, in Devizes Castle, secure and surrounded by his loyal court in the care of the papal legate, a very apprehensive young boy king bit his nails as he waited to hear the outcome of this decisive battle for his crown. William Marshal from the Dover cliff tops could see clearly the lines of Blanche of Castile's fleet, commanded by the piratical Eustace the Monk, approaching in the distance. According to one eye witness,

> So dense was the fleet and in such good order that it was like a pitched battle. In advance proceeded the ship of Eustace the Monk, the great ship of Bayonne, who was its guide and master, and which contained the treasure of the king.[2]

The Cinque Ports sailors could see them too and when, at about eighty, they lost count of the French ships, many of them started to reconsider fishing as a better option and made to take their ships back to port. But Marshal, using his powers of persuasion, and potently describing the chances of taking a vast amount of treasure from the French fleet, converted their thinking and the mariners fell in behind Hubert's leading ship as he, with no recorded sea captaincy experience, set out from Sandwich to adapt his castellan's belligerent skills to a maritime environment. But before finally leaving the quayside Hubert had loaded various offensive materials that he hoped to put to effective use if the battle went in his favour. The importance of the French relief expeditionary force can be gauged by the seniority of its commanders. Sailing on the flagship with Eustace the Monk were, for example, Robert de Courtenay a cousin of Louis, and Nevelon de Chanle, son of the castellan of Arras, also senior nobility such as Ralph de la Tourniele, Guillaume le Maréchal and William des Barres. Eight large troop and equipment carriers held some 125 knights leading the force of thousands of men at arms, supported by scores of lesser supplies vessels and, not least an assortment of mercenary piratical ruffians out for whatever they could get. Also on board was millions in coin and bullion treasure; the war horses for the knights; and, not least, a state-of-the-art trebuchet catapult for destroying Dover.

Hubert sailed his ship ahead of the Cinque Ports fleet to feint an attack, but then put about away from the French lines in an apparently non-combatant manoeuvre; but Hubert had gained his ships the weather-gage, the prevailing wind now blowing from Hubert's flotilla towards Eustace's ships. His fleet followed him in line astern. The French, heading towards the Thames Estuary, made to ignore the English fleet apparently now going the other way. But French battle commander, Robert de Courtenay, had doubts and, deciding otherwise, he heeled his ship over to engage the nearest English vessel. To avoid a collision, Eustace's ship had to swing away, but then struck the second ship of the English column commanded by Richard FitzJohn. Hubert's ship was ahead of the collision but seeing the confusion, he then came about and trapped Eustace's ship between his own and Fitzjohn's. Two other English ships completed the sandwich and Robert de Courtenay was soon swimming for his life. The French fleet, now in disarray, all started to join battle with Hubert's fleet: but now Hubert could make best use of his cogs. These made for Eustace's now static ship and from their castle decks opened casks of unslaked powdered lime (Hubert's secret weapon) and threw it into the easterly wind, taking the blinding clouds over the French vessels. Jumping down from his cog into a French ship, one Ranulf Paganus landed in a group of blinded French knights, scattering them. The rest of the ship's company followed him taking prisoner thirty-two knights. Ships with their rigging slashed by the English were targeted by Hubert's crossbowmen who picked off the entangled French like birds in a net. On board Eustace's Great Ship of Bayonne the hunt was on for Eustace himself who had seemingly disappeared. Eventually he was found cowering in the bilges and was hauled on deck by Cinque Ports seaman Stephen Crabbe of Winchelsea. Eustace started bargaining for his life, but it was to the wrong man. Crabbe had suffered Eustace's attacks many times and now offered him two alternatives – beheading on the gunwales, or on the trebuchet stored on deck. The choice we do not know, the outcome we do, and Stephen Crabbe continued the fight with his cutlass in one hand and Eustace's head in the other.

Across the sea battle arena similar scenes were enacted as the French fleet was smashed by the English, the great galleys piercing their armoured prows into the fat-bellied supply transports. The sea was awash with blood and bodies as the English started to take in tow their lucrative prize ships and return to Sandwich and Dover from which shoreline and clifftops thousands had watched the progression of the battle. Just 32 out of a probable 125 French knights survived and were taken hostage for high value ransoms, while one contemporary annalist vividly stated that the French:

were run through by bolts and arrows, pierced by spears, had their throats cut by knives and were cut to pieces by swords ... a good four thousand men were killed, without counting those who leapt into the sea and were drowned.[3]

While historian Richard Hakluyt (1553–1616) later succinctly observed, 'Hubert armed fortee tall ships and meeting with eightie sail of French men upon the high seas, gave them a most courageous encounter in which he tooke some, sunke others and discomfited the rest.'

The remnants of the French attempted to limp back to Calais but many were caught by the faster English ships and sunk, just a handful made it there to give Blanche of Castile the news that her son's cause in England was now lost. Hubert himself returned to Dover with two prize vessels in tow to be met with a hero's welcome from a joyful populace headed by William Marshal. After much thanksgiving at an impromptu quayside service, Philip d'Aubigny was despatched to Devizes to take the great news to the Royalist court waiting there in considerable apprehension. Meanwhile the head of Eustace the Monk was paraded in triumph to Canterbury and thence through the south to London. Religious thought dominated much of medieval daily life and it is no surprise that Hubert and other leaders wished to use some of the treasure they had taken ('sharing out coin by the shovel-full' recorded one chronicler) to erect a religious memorial to the battle. Consequently, in Sandwich they built a chapel dedicated to St Bartholomew on whose day and with whose aid they attributed the victory. The buildings survive to this day.[4] As indeed does the annual dedication service held there to St Bartholomew: it is thought to be the oldest such service performed in the country.

This English victory, the first after the Norman Conquest in a Channel battle, won against great odds over the French by Hubert de Burgh off Sandwich, has been lost to modern memory: hopefully this narrative will go some way towards recovering that lapse. If looked at in finer detail it might be construed an even greater national victory than that of the 1588 Armada. Then there was little practical chance of a Spanish force succeeding much beyond a beach landing from which they would have been repulsed by an overpowering land army; whereas in 1217 much of southern England,

London, and the eastern Home Counties had been occupied by French forces for a year and a half. Although John's premature death started to alter the balance against Louis, it cannot be taken for granted that had Blanche's Sandwich fleet of reinforcements made a successful landfall, and then joined up with the occupation force in its London HQ and utilized their resources to the best advantage, the largely mercenary English force might not have held the country. At least one contemporary chronicler agrees,

> She [Blanche] went at her task so energetically that if all those she assembled had come in arms to London, they would have conquered the whole kingdom.[5]

Hubert de Burgh's inspired leadership on the day ensured it never came to this ultimate test and the Battle of Sandwich, 1217, must stand as the first in our history of the great defensive encounters fought out in the Channel waters against outnumbering odds. A foremost modern naval historian concurs:

> Fought under way, in an age when naval battles were usually stationary, it displays a precocious grasp of naval tactics by Hubert de Burgh which was hardly equalled by any other English admiral before the sixteenth century.[6]

Indeed it might not be too far-fetched to identify the events of St Bartholomew's Day, 1217, as a medieval manifestation of 'the Few' of 1940, and fought out in the identical arena. It was certainly the first of the many Channel naval battles between the French and English.

All pretence to the English throne had been abandoned by Louis and, with the dust of battle now settled, William Marshal, Hubert de Burgh, the papal legate Cardinal Gualo, with other governing regency courtiers, made the political facts of life crystal clear to Louis at a conference held during the first week in September in the Chapter House of Merton Priory. The formal signing of the negotiated peace treaty took place afterwards on 12 September 1217, on a Thames islet at nearby Kingston-upon-Thames. A conciliatory golden handshake was agreed to allow Louis to leave England, with his residual forces, while still preserving some favour in the eyes of his father Philip's court, watching events from across the Channel. The English regency knew well that they needed to keep the European courts onside for the restabilization process still to be undertaken. One of the provisions of the Kingston-upon-Thames treaty had been to give Hubert carte blanche to use as he thought best the revenues of his many shrievalties in restoring Dover castle, now recognized as the country's most tactically important fortress. This agreement ran to 1221 after which it was superseded by a flat rate of £1,000 p.a. made available from the Treasury. The London citizenry were persuaded to change their allegiance to the young King Henry, any opposing French officials promptly being put on the next boat home.

In December 1217 a 'tidying up' operation over the ensuing weeks across the midlands and the south kick-started an imposition of the regency's authority: this saw Hubert gathering at Dover hapless French prisoners apprehended trying to live off the countryside. He negotiated their exchange (plus a 100 marks ransom if possible) for various Englishmen that King Philip had found in France in suspicious circumstances and similarly taken into custody. While this was happening Hubert took time at Dover to oversee repairs to his castle, replacing the damaged wooden outer defences to the north with the stone curtain walling that still stands today. The help given to the Royalist forces by the guerrilla leader in the Wealden forests, William de Cassingham, was not overlooked either. John had, in September 1216, written him a letter of appreciation. Henry too, after the war, reiterated his father's and added his own thanks for the critical importance of William's role in keeping the French coastal lines of communication cut and in killing thousands of the enemy in the Wealden forests. William was granted a property, defined as the Seven Hundreds of the Weald, a government pension for his lifetime and, when he predeceased his wife, she continued to receive a Treasury benefit for another seven years.[7]

Hubert had his own celebration during this September in his marriage to Isabella, Countess of Gloucester, one of the richest heiresses in England. He had known her for years, from the time she was married to John when Count of Mortain, but the latter had, on his accession to the throne, divorced her. Now Hubert by his second marriage hoped to gain title to her vast estates across the country. But the best laid plans … the unfortunate Isabella died

Dover Castle. For his implacable, undefeated defence of this 'key to the kingdom', Hubert de Burgh was made Earl of Kent. (*BLOM*)

The four momentous Plantagenet kings, with 'The Young Henry' in the centre. Henry II (top left), Richard I (top right), John (bottom left) and Henry III. (*British Library, MS Roy.14 C VII f.9*)

Hubert de Burgh's men-at-arms despatching the piratical French Admiral, Eustace the Monk, on the gunwales of Eustace's own *Great Ship of Bayonne* during the Battle of Sandwich, 24 August 1217. (*Matthew Paris MS 16. Folio 52, Corpus Christi College, Cambridge*)

The head of pirate Eustace the Monk being paraded through Canterbury after the defeat of the French fleet off Sandwich by Hubert de Burgh, 24 August 1217. (*Mary Evans Picture Library*)

A crossbowman arming his weapon. (*British Library, Addn MS 42130, f.56*)

'A mail-clad Plantagenet knight draws his sword.' (*Lutterworth Press*, A Knight and his Armour, *1961*)

Prince Louis of France and his generals arriving to invade England. (*Corpus Christi, Cambridge, MS 016 f.46v*)

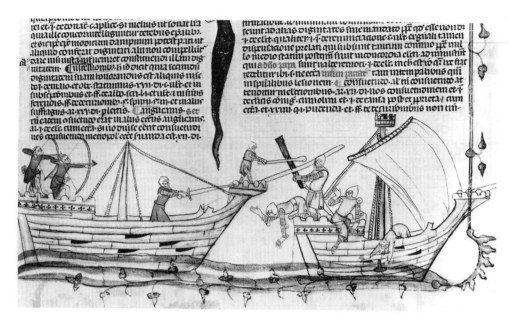

Cogs in Battle. Their distinctive fore and aft castles clearly seen. (*British Library*)

Château Gaillard. Richard the Lionheart's 'Saucy Castle' on the Seine at Les Andelys. It fell with little resistance to King Philip of France in 1203. (*France Tourisme*)

Rochester Castle. After Hubert de Burgh undermined the keep in November 1215, the present Poitevin cylindrical tower replaced it. (*English Heritage*)

John 'Softsword' with his dogs. When not terrorising his subjects, John was following the hounds in one of his many royal forests. There still remain various 'King John's Hunting Lodge' buildings in today's residual forested areas. (*British Library, MS Roy 20 A II*)

King John considering his fate after sealing Magna Charta at Runnymede on 10 June 1215. (*M. Dovaston*, Story of the British Nation Vol. 1, *385*, Hutchinson *1922*)

Falaise Castle. At Falaise in April 1203 King John murdered Prince Arthur of Brittany, the rightful heir to the English throne. (*Marianne Majerus*)

The murder of Prince Arthur of Brittany, heir to the English throne, in April 1203, as imagined by William Shakespeare in his *The Tragedie of King John.* Here Hubert is portrayed by the great John Kemble in the 1790s. (*J. Rogers/W. Hamilton* (*Mary Evans*))

Chinon Castle. Hubert defended this massive fortress against a French army for eighteen months until June 1205. (*France Tourisme*)

Donjon de Niort. Hubert's operational headquarters when Seneschal of Poitou, 1213–15. It was never besieged. (*France Tourisme*)

The Battle of Bouvines Bridge. The victory here of the French over the combined British force on 27 July 1214 marked the beginning of the end for English continental ambitions. (*Bibliothèque Nationale, Ms Français 2609, f.219v*)

Plan of the Anglo Angevin continental provinces. After the Battle of Bouvines this Angevin empire quickly disintegrated. (*The Struggle for Mastery: Britain 1066–1284, p.xii, D. Carpenter, Allen Lane, 2003*)

Old St Paul's (1085–1666) much as Hubert saw it. It dominated London's skyline as does the Shard today. (*The Builder Ltd.,1962*)

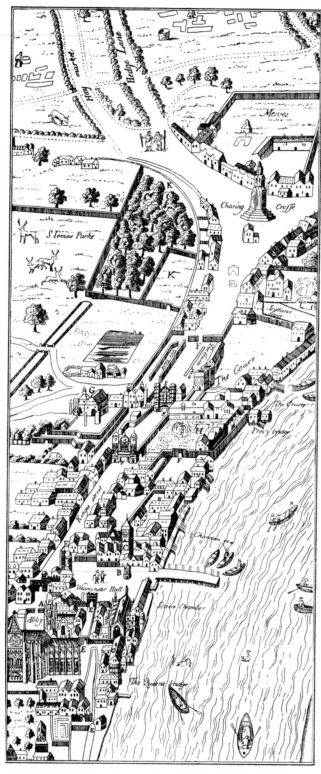

Whitehall Palace c1570 by Ralph Agas. It grew from Hubert de Burgh's Thames-side mansion and would eventually cover 23 acres. (*Museum of London*)

Hadleigh Castle in Essex. Built in the 1220s by Hubert de Burgh as his early warning fortification against Thames estuary incursions into his homeland. (*English Heritage*)

Creake Abbey. Founded in 1206 by Sir Robert and Lady Alice of Nerford, Hubert's East Anglian neighbours. It was granted Abbey status in October 1231 through Hubert's influence. Sir Robert was Hubert's deputy fleet commander at the Battle of Sandwich. (*English Heritage*)

Self-portrait of Matthew Paris, St Alban's monk and Hubert's oldest friend and confidant. (*British Library*)

Hubert de Burgh depicted in sanctuary at Merton Priory where Hubert stayed in hiding from King John's 'hit squad' during July 1232. (*British Library, Matthew Paris Historia Anglorum, Roy.14.C.VII. fol.119v*)

The original Norman gateway of Merton Priory. Hubert de Burgh would have passed through it many times. (*Merton Council*)

Magna Charta. The best preserved of the
four surviving copies of the document.
(*British Library Cot. MS Augustus II 106*)

Skenfrith Castle in Monmouthshire, the most used of Hubert de Burgh's 'Three Castles of the Justiciar'. The other two were nearby Grosmont and White Castle. (*CADW: Welsh Historic Monuments*)

Skenfrith Castle. A reconstruction of how it looked in Hubert's time. (*CADW: Chris Jones-Jenkins*)

The Seal of Winchelsea. The ship – an improved version of the Cog – is weighing anchor and setting sail, with trumpeters sounding the departure. (*National Maritime Museum, Greenwich*)

Second coronation of Henry III, taking place at Westminster Abbey on 17 May 1220. Henry is still the only English monarch to have two coronations. (*Cambridge, Corpus Christi College 16, fol.56*)

A thirteenth-century Gascony wine jug – a drinking vessel very familiar to Hubert de Burgh. (*Carisbrooke Castle Museum, I.O.W./English Heritage*)

St Bartholomew's Chapel, Sandwich, Kent. Built in 1217 by the Sandwich parishioners with the treasure taken from the French fleet defeated by Hubert de Burgh on 24 August – St Bartholomew's Day. (*1917 Postcard*)

The late twelfth-century murals at the Chapelle Sainte-Radegonde at Chinon Castle. Henry II and Queen Eleanour are depicted, but other family identities are open to question.

just a month later and Hubert was unable to assume the inheritance, her lands as a royal peeress reverting to the crown.

As the 'Merton Priory' mentioned above was to be of vital, indeed life-saving, importance to Hubert in later years, a short description of this great and ancient foundation will not be out of place here. This Augustinian Priory (in south-east London) was founded by Gilbert the Norman, who was Sheriff both of Surrey and of Huntingdon and to whom Henry I had granted the Manor of Merton in about 1114. Henry had then invited the Prior of Huntingdon Priory to found a cell in Merton. By the thirteenth century Merton Priory managed some two hundred manors spread over sixteen counties, not to mention the continual upkeep of its adjoining River Effra. It had consequently grown in size to 65 acres with its church having a nave of 330ft length. The priors eventually failed to manage such a weighty property portfolio, and inferior husbandry and declining revenues combined to consign it to the national Dissolution in 1538. Its famous educational base – from which had emerged such alumni as Nicholas Breakspear, England's only Pope (Adrian IV), Thomas à Becket, also Walter de Merton, one-time Chancellor of England – had also degenerated. As one of the Priory's most distinguished benefactors, Walter de Merton founded in 1264 the nearby 'House of the Scholars of Merton'. His foundation was later transferred to Oxford in 1274 where, now as Merton, it claims to be the university's oldest college: it certainly houses the oldest recognized academic university library in the world, founded in 1373. In its heyday the Merton monks kept a suite of rooms for the monarch, should one wish to call in – Henry III did on occasion, Henry I also – but in his coffin, lying in state. The Dissolution saw the Priory torn down and the stones sent to Henry VIII's nearby ill-fated Nonsuch castle project. But most of the original Priory main entrance gate survives at Merton, now re-erected in the parish church precincts – it is the same one Hubert would have known and passed through many times. Also visible today are the original foundations of the Chapter House which was witness to many major moments and decisions of English history – as above described. Perhaps one of the Priory's strangest occurrences was the purchase of a manor house there on 4 June 1668, by Thomas Pepys, cousin of the great diarist. Said Samuel on the day 'which is a mistake I am sorry for'. The diarist detested his cousin, 'a sorry dull fellow he is, fit for nothing that is ingenious; nor is there a turd of kindness or service to be had from him'. Thomas died at Merton in 1675.

(In 2014 the 750th anniversary of their College was celebrated by the Oxford Mertonians with a three-day long summer 'Birthday Weekend'.)

Chapter 10

1217–1221 Recovery of the Realm

The departure of the French allowed the regency council to concentrate its corporate mind on the anarchic state of the country. Both regent William Marshal, and papal legate Gualo, looked to Hubert de Burgh as Justiciar and as such, national head of law and order to co-ordinate their efforts for the reinstatement of civil obedience. This dedicated triumvirate made the first move towards stability with Henry III's first official entry into London to participate in a Great Council set up in late October to further revise Magna Charta by removing the residual points of contention which had alienated the barons. On 6 November 1217 the council reached its agreement on the new format, the principal difference being that the laws of the royal forests were deemed important enough to require their own Charter. Sealed on that date by both regent and papal legate, the new Charter removed the forest clauses from the 1215 and 1216 Charters and set them out anew in the 'Forest Charter': the three original 1215 forest clauses becoming 17 in 1217. The non-forest clauses continued as the 'Magna Charta', it being so-called as being the larger of the two new documents. The implementation of the 'Forest Charter' was assigned to the responsibility of the regent's son, the highly competent John Marshal. Only one copy of the 1216 Charter survives, in Durham Cathedral. However, three originals of the 1217 Charter survive in the Bodleian Library, Oxford University; one came from Gloucester Abbey, and two from Oseney Abbey, while one exemplar is at Durham Cathedral. Another stalwart from earlier times also had a lifelong interest in helping draft the Forest Charter terms – Hugh de Neville, the King's forester. A valiant Crusader with Richard the Lionheart, de Neville, as a reward for his bravery, was given charge of the royal forests. He continued in this post under John and, with John Marshal, jointly managed the tens of thousands of acres of royal forests across many counties. Hugh de Neville, friend of Hubert and man of many anecdotes, was married to Joan de Cornhill, daughter of Henry of Cornhill, and Joan had been a favourite mistress of John. Then down in the forests something stirred ... An entry in the official Chancery Records for 1204 reveals that after a sojourn with John the King asked Joan what it would be worth for her to go back to sleeping with her husband – the annalist (delightfully?) records her answer as being '200 chickens!'. Along the borders of the realm stability was maintained as, during December 1217, the King of the Scots, Alexander II, officially recognized the regency. Then the leader of the Welsh, Llywelwyn ab Iorwerth, at the Council of Worcester in March 1218, agreed the surrender of royal castles and lands he had taken during John's attacks on the principality. A further measure aimed at controlling lawlessness, and potentially warlike behaviour by egotistic knights, was the regency's banning of Tournaments.

The year 1218 was one of great personal achievement for Hubert. Travelling with his now considerable personal staff around the country in his Justiciar's role he set in place many revised laws of tenure to right the wrongs in property appropriation suffered by the general public under the hated John. Additionally, he appointed the holding of assizes in most counties to settle local disputes according to the provisions of the newly operative latest version of Magna Charta. At the same time his countrywide progress allowed the public to put a face to the name, for by now Hubert was a nationally famous figure and those people with whom he came into contact felt that the recovery of law and order was back in safe hands once more and, most importantly, those hands were of native English, not continental origin. Hubert was also at this time in attendance on the new Exchequer courts set up to recover the country's financial stability. He consistently sat at meetings about financial measures introduced consequent upon his decisions as Justiciar: he was to exert substantial personal influence on Exchequer decisions and reform for some years after the war. During Hubert's absences from Dover the governorship of the castle there devolved upon his deputy, his uncle, Sir Robert de Nereford, a relative from Hubert's East Anglian homeland. And, in fact, the regulations for the government of the castle that Hubert drew up at this time continued largely unchanged for another three centuries. He again continued to amass shrievalties, and honours of land as he had done during John's reign; not a few of these were bribes to regain his favour with magnates who had been on the wrong side during the French occupation. As a consequence during that autumn Hubert received one gift of property that he would cherish for the rest of his life. One of the former rebels, William de Mowbray, made over the ownership of his country estate at Banstead in Surrey to Hubert during the autumn of 1218 – probably as a means of keeping in the Justiciar's good books during the latter's judicial decisions on rebels and their estates. It was to become Hubert's favourite 'place in the country' and which, according to John Aubrey visiting Banstead in the 1670s, offered,

> a stately prospect into Kent, Hertfordshire, Middlesex, Buckinghamshire, part of Oxfordshire, Hampshire, Berkshire, and a full view of the City of London from the Tower to Westminster.[1]

When his responsibilities allowed, Hubert liked nothing better than to relax there; high up on the North Downs, enjoying the view over much of the southern counties, considering his options, thinking out his national policies, with his fine cellar of the best Bordeaux vintages, and no doubt a goblet of one to hand. That view from those Surrey hilltops remains breathtaking today, we can only guess how evocatively British it must have looked to Hubert when pristine all those years ago. But what a wonderful comparison is conjured up when we realize that less than ten miles to the east of Banstead, atop the same outcrop in the Surrey Hills, exactly seven centuries later, another national leader, Sir Winston Churchill, would also gaze out from his country retreat at Chartwell across that selfsame view enjoyed by Hubert. His thinking too, c.1940, was dominated by foreign interference in English life – and with a tasty glass to hand on occasion. The parallels are compelling: both men fought their country's cause abroad, both were taken prisoner-of-war overseas, both saviours of their nation in the arena of the Channel against seemingly overpowering odds, both marrying a wife from another country, both political movers and shakers of the highest order, both chief advisors on national defence to their monarchs, and the one initiating the role of Cinque Ports Guardian that the other would inherit as Lord Warden. It is more than likely too that, in his Banstead seclusion, Hubert organized networking meetings with his friends and allies, both in country and Court, to work out their policies and survival plans within that acidic Angevin regime. Maybe such gatherings were tempered with good-natured tussles at 'bac gamen' boards, as the drink, conversation, and planning flowed.

One option for which Hubert sought redress during this period was his claim to the castellanship of the Three Castles in the Welsh Marches: John had deprived him of them in 1205 during Hubert's captivity after Chinon and given them to the custody of Reginald de Braose, a powerful border lord. But the King's court at Westminster adjudged Hubert the rightful claimant – he had produced John's charter to him as evidence before the court and de Braose had not come to Westminster to defend his acquisition. Hubert was granted back his key castle group in January 1219 and very soon after was visiting the Sheriff of Herefordshire to tell him about the accommodation improvements and defensive updating he was going to put in hand at Skenfrith and Grosmont. He left Whitecastle to a later date, preferring to keep it as a supplies base for the other two.[2]

Back in London momentous events were in train, the papal legate Gualo had returned to Rome to be replaced by Pandulf, who had previously attended John's court between 1211–1215. Also, shortly after the legate's arrival, on 14 May 1219, Hubert would have received the news that, not very distant from his Banstead estate, the great William Marshal, Earl of Pembroke and regent, had died at his Caversham estate. He was given a full Templars' funeral with all its heraldic trappings. His mortal remains were caparisoned with the Mantle of the Templars laid on the coffin by Aimery de St Maur, Master of the Order, and taken first to Reading Abbey for a full Mass, then on arrival in London, another Mass was performed at Westminster Abbey, finally he was laid to rest in the circular Templar's Church, off Fleet Street. There is little doubt that, in the future, Hubert found some private time to visit that Fleet Street church to stand at the tomb of his lifelong comrade-in-arms, friend, and bravest-of-the-brave Crusader. There, in tearful memory, and leaning heavily on Margaret's now ever-present arm, the grizzled veteran shuffled back his thoughts in silent soliloquy over the years – Chinon, Magna Charta, the Battle of Lincoln, defence of Dover, the sea victory over the French at Sandwich, the Regency years ... All world changing events and times through which they stood together against unmeasured odds. After their visit, when Hubert and Margaret turned and left the Templar's Church, Hubert's eye may have been caught by a carved stone just outside the door; looking closely he would read that it commemorated the consecration of the church in 1185 by Patriarch Heraclius of Jerusalem. Stopping in his tracks, that date would have brought home to Hubert all he had achieved in the thirty-four years since he first came to London to be a courtier. William Marshal's effigy tomb continues today to attract thousands of annual visitors – probably too, on occasions, the ghost of Hubert de Burgh mingles amongst them.

The Poitevin Bishop of Winchester, Peter des Roches, had been hoping to take the place of Marshal as regent, but agreement had been made that Pandulf assume the role, and so it was. The effect of the decision was to make Peter and Hubert side by side councillors answerable only to the regent vice the young King; as destiny yoked them together they were effectively going to be running the country, though their opposing nationalities, viewpoints and enmity made them impossible bedfellows. The fact that royal letters from April 1219 were predominantly witnessed by Hubert de Burgh and issued under his seal, not a royal one, indicates his predominance over the Poitevin.[3] And Peter des Roches always was to hold that Hubert had influenced the choice of Pandulf against him. Quite likely Hubert had, but if so he probably wasn't alone, for another anonymous contemporary records that Peter des Roches was widely disliked and seen to be 'sharp at accounting, slack at scriptures'.[4] At this time too, in February, 1219, occurs evidence that Hubert had once considered going on the Fifth Crusade, for the papal records hold his letter asking dispensation from his vow, 'inasmuch as his absence would be ruinous to the castles and fortresses, especially that of Dover, of which he is a sworn governor'.[5]

During 1219 negotiations were held with the now relatively quiescent French to extend the truce which had commenced in 1214 when John had made the kingdom a papal vassal. His death annulled the Vatican's imposition of papal rule and now Pandulf took steps to ensure Philip had no cause to challenge the regency. Consequently, a peace treaty effective from 3 March 1220 was signed by the Archbishop of Canterbury, the Bishop of Winchester, Hubert de Burgh, Earl Warrenne and the Earl of Salisbury. To underpin the political stability of the treaty vis-à-vis English interests on the continent,

Hubert was asked to recommend a seneschal to be sent to Aquitaine. His choice was Hugh de Vivonne, who had been refusing to give up lands he had taken from the Earl of Gloucester during the war. Hubert was following his own private agenda in keeping favour with the great and ancient Gloucester de Clare family by ridding them of the troublesome Poitevin.

It was doubtless commented on at the time, and Hubert would certainly have known that, in 1220, when he received his summons to attend the second coronation of Henry on 17 May, no other English monarch had ever had two coronations. But thus it was with Henry III at Westminster Abbey on that day, to further progress the recovery of the realm and to make public the act of accession which had not been practical at Gloucester during the war. To this day Henry III remains the only English monarch to have had two coronations. Henry's was the last coronation in the old Westminster Abbey: the previous day he had ceremoniously laid the first stone of the Lady Chapel of the present building which he dedicated to Edward the Confessor. Meanwhile, another member of the de Burghs was quietly carving out his own niche in national history at this time. Young Richard, eldest son of Hubert's late brother William, was appointed to the governing council of the Irish Justiciar in 1220. At a later date he would accede to that highest office himself. Hubert of course pulled all possible strings at court to ease his nephew's path to success. Hubert's help would certainly have been gratefully received as Richard continued to grapple with the political aftermath of the infamous 'Laudabiliter' measure imposed on Ireland in 1155 by Pope Adrian IV (the English Pope). Effectively this had given Henry II the right to rule Ireland ecclesiastically. The Irish kings of Munster, Leinster, Meath, Ulster and Connaught disagreed. The reverberations continue today.

A complex medieval tradition involved monarchs using their unmarried daughters as bargaining pieces when cementation of political agreements at the highest level took place. The daughter (plus a dowry) would be offered in engagement to the suitor with the subsequent marriage occurring at a time and place of the recipient party's choosing. The betrothal could, and often did, extend for years, the girls being, as it were, kept in reserve for the contracted man. In actuality much could happen to complicate things in the interim: so it was to be with Hubert. Back in 1209 the Scots King William the Lion had signed a peace treaty with John under which he gave his two daughters to the pleasure of the English King, plus a dowry of 15,000 marks. John pocketed the dowry for himself and assigned the eldest girl to his heir. Now a decade later in 1220, a new agreement was negotiated by the regency which released the elder daughter Margaret from this obligation to marry Henry, there being no perceived political advantage now. Meanwhile Henry's sister Joan became affianced to Alexander, the new Scots King, and son of William the Lion. They were married in June 1221 at York Minster. Hubert went along and, as always, with an eye to the main chance, set his hat at the newly freed Margaret of Scotland. She assented to his advances, and why not? Out of nowhere the chance to become the wife of one of the English King's closest circle, a castellan to several royal castles and over a score of lesser ones, with extensive estates across many counties, plus lucrative interests in the vineyards of Bordeaux, and honoured as an English national hero. The midges and mountains, puddles and porridge of Scotland versus the high life of southern England with perhaps trips abroad to the sun – the young Margaret (she was approaching 30 and Hubert nearing 50) wasn't going to get a better offer!

Hubert of course had taken other factors into account, his standing at court not least: now he would be the brother-in-law of the King of Scotland, a much enhanced profile for the ambitious Justiciar. Hubert and Margaret were married at the great Church of Holy Trinity in London in the September of 1221 by Archbishop of Canterbury Stephen Langton, in a lavish ceremony which included everybody who was anybody. Might Hubert, we wonder, have experienced that same momentary déjà-vu twinge he felt as he passed the Holy Trinity Priory that day when he first came to London some thirty-five years ago? It could be thought that Hubert in his marriage was seeing things at an international level which others might not have. What better way to help fix a long-lasting Anglo/Scots peace than for two of the most senior court members from opposing sides of Hadrian's Wall to join in marriage and in so doing help keep that fractious border more settled. Hubert saw only a win/win outcome for his, his King's, and the Scots King's international responsibilities – and he had the prospect of the whole new experience of home life with a loving wife. (How different from the Anglo/Scots angst of 2014!) While these happy events occupied the news of the day another significant occurrence was the return of Pandulf, the papal legate, to Rome. He was not replaced, Stephen Langton as Archbishop of Canterbury assuming the role as Rome's representative in England. However, Archbishop Langton had long been aware of his Justiciar's prominence in governmental administration and was therefore happy to allow Hubert to witness royal writs, keep the judicial system up to date, and even exercise some supervision of the Exchequer. But Pandulf, consummate diplomat as he was, on his way back to Rome, spent some time in the Norman provinces on a hearts and minds campaign. He visited Aquitaine where he met with Hugh de Lusignan, the now unquestioned leader of Poitou, and forged a peace agreement to run for the next two years. To buttress this agreement he promoted the elevation to Seneschal of Poitou and Gascony of Savary de Mauleon. This disciplined role kept the erstwhile loose cannon Savary within the bounds of the law.

In between exercising his top-level national responsibilities, Hubert occupied himself in touring many of his landholdings, castles, and mansions across the country. Although held in his personal name, they were all run by under-sheriffs and bailiffs: his vast East Anglian estates across Norfolk, Suffolk, and Essex, were managed by Richard de Fresingfield; in Kent Hugh de Windsor reported to him, but Dover Castle he entrusted separately to Robert de Nereford, his family relative from Norfolk. Hubert was well versed in the fiscal duties attached to being sheriff, and he now worked effortlessly between national and local government; also he knew everyone who was anyone and never ran out of favours owed to him. Everyone ambitious for court favour wanted a piece of the political aura which Hubert's personal presence exuded like some heady incense. As an example, an alliance of knights from Nottinghamshire sent him a gift (bribe?) of a vast amount of local timber with which to improve and extend his family mansion at Burgh in Norfolk. Hubert didn't accept all gifts and favours offered, but just those he thought would most benefit his own aims – and he would remember who those donors were.

Chapter 11

1221–1226 King in all but Name

Hubert de Burgh now entered an era where he was virtually able to rule the country: however, opposition to him in this role was not to be long in coming. He had of course to work hand in hand with his close confidant, Archbishop of Canterbury, Stephen Langton, and on occasions when he didn't, the Angevin opposition was quick to pounce! An early test of his resilience under political personal pressure occurred at Winchester during the King's Christmas gathering there at the end of 1221. While the party was in full swing the Justiciar and the Earl of Salisbury got involved in a heated quarrel with his old adversary Ranulph, Earl of Chester, and Falkes de Breaute, the illegitimate son of a Norman knight. A favourite of John, Falkes de Breaute had held several royal castellanships in the east Midlands, and even among the Angevins, was exceptionally ruthless and unscrupulous. Now, only the intervention of Stephen Langton and the publicly announced threat of excommunication to all antagonists halted the altercation, but everyone present knew that sides were going to have to be taken as Hubert's new administration advanced in its aims. And the young King took note too. Nevertheless, by the following summer Hubert was beginning to find his authority unassailable and this he demonstrated in London when sent to the capital to sort out a riot between some men of Westminster and others from the City of London, both supporting an annual contest of athletic ability. After all concerned had had too much to drink, some extensive vandalism was inflicted upon the property of the Abbot of Westminster, but more seriously the mobs concerned were haranguing the hapless local authorities with chants sympathetic to the late French cause. (Louis had of course controlled his invasion from a compliant London government for nearly two years.) Roger of Wendover gives his account,

On the day of St James the Apostle, the citizens of the city of London met outside the city to engage in wrestling with the citizens of the suburban districts to see which of them possessed the greatest strength. After they had contended for a long time amidst the shouts of both parties, the Londoners, having put their antagonists into disorder gained the victory. The Seneschal of Westminster, however, with his suburban companions and fellow provincials, who sought revenge rather than sport, without any reason, flew to arms and severely beat the Londoners who had come there unarmed, causing bloodshed among them. The citizens, shamefully wounded, retreated to the city in great confusion. After they had got into the city, a tumult arose among the populace. The irrational mob, with others of the city, went forth in disorder with Constantine at their head, and embarked upon a civil uprising.

At this point Matthew Paris added to Roger's account 'The said Constantine called out in a loud voice, as a sort of rallying cry, "Mont-joie, Mont-joie! May the Lord assist us and our Lord Louis!" And this greatly exasperated the friends of the king and provoked them to take vengeance.'

Upon his arrival on the scene with his troops Hubert arrested the leaders, Constantine FitzAluph and others, had them executed the following day, took hostages for the future good behaviour of both sides, and dismissed from office the city mayor and aldermen for not having used their authority with sufficient force to prevent the situation deteriorating as it did. But many influential Londoners saw Hubert's treatment of the dissidents as draconian and a clandestine anti-Justiciar movement started to take root. Their attitude was backed also by a well-founded tradition arising from a statement made in 1135 that only the City of London could choose a King of England.[1] Although Hubert ignored this supposed precedent, he would be reminded of his uncompromising actions on this day at a future time. Meanwhile, any event likely to create a crowd with militant tendencies was banned by Hubert's laws. It had been a popular pastime to hold tournaments between local teams, these were now made unlawful and if held privately could result in the sponsors having their lands forfeited to the crown. Although having spent much of his life at the sharp end of war and conflict Hubert, as now the country's senior statesman, sought to make his homeland as peaceable as his abilities (and enemies) allowed.

At this time Hubert had his attention turned back to Ireland with its seemingly endless fiscal and political problems. Justiciar of the province, Geoffrey de Marsh, had been caught with his hand in the provincial till. Summoned back by Hubert in August 1220 to account for his actions, Geoffrey was put on a good behaviour warning and told he could only retain his post under the supervision of a committee comprising the Archbishop of Dublin, a royal clerk Thomas Fitz Adam, and Richard de Burgh. The hapless Geoffrey's habit proved too ingrained and within a year he was on his way to an early retirement. The committee however successfully continued in its supervisory role over the Irish finances, with Hubert's young nephew Richard taking a large step up the ladder of national responsibility which would culminate in his becoming Justiciar of Ireland.

Being Justiciar meant Hubert had to maintain a close and detailed knowledge of the laws of the land, though he did of course have his own team of attorneys which kept him up to date with the latest rulings likely to lead to disputes and, equally, settlements of civil cases. As a consequence a passage of litigation which occurred in July 1222 was a historical event. It concerned the term 'limit of legal memory' and it was the basis of claims of *writ mort d'ancestor*. In short this right had been established in 1176 from the Northampton Assizes, and it allowed the tenant's heirs a claim on the property on the death of the tenant. The litigation approved by Hubert defined the 'limit of legal memory' to be from the accession of Henry II to the accession of Richard I. This law as signified by Hubert, and updated by regnal periods as it went along, stood until 1833.

Hubert had a great responsibility in the fiscal duties of his office; the royal castles for instance needed continuous income to keep them in state-of-the-art defensive condition. To this end one of his far-reaching measures was to bring under royal control the income from the county shrievalty that John had allowed to lapse during his reign in order to keep favour with the barons concerned. According to one authority[2] the annual Exchequer receipts resulting from this revision for 1222 amounted to £33,443.17.3 against a pre-Hubert annual average of £28,000. Hubert applied the law stringently, in both military and fiscal terms, to the greater benefit of the land. He also gave himself a pay rise – to £300 p.a. from December 1222.[3]

In the exercise of his responsibilities Hubert de Burgh did not of course work from Westminster on his own, the two archbishops, Canterbury and York, together with the other pre-eminent bishops of the land, Winchester, Durham, Salisbury, London, the Treasurer Eustace de Faucenburg, and, as well, the most senior dukes and earls, all had some say on the various councils through which Hubert exercised his authority, but in the end few came up with better ways of handling the ongoing problems in hand. Hubert was not a prevaricator, or compromiser, instead he was very much a seat-of-the-pants decision maker in much of what he decided upon. On most of the surviving royal documents of this time he appears as the principal witness and signatory, effectively leading the young King Henry from behind. He made mistakes of course, as when on 30 January 1223 he asked for returns from the county sheriffs listing the social and fiscal customs in operation in the shires before the war, and he wanted answers by 8 May! All recipients revolted against this imposition and Hubert was forced to defer to Archbishop Langton's advice and revise the effective date of his memo to end-June. But in the end its mandatory nature became watered down, the returns being eventually made on an 'as and when' basis. Interestingly, Hubert's administration seems to have accumulated sufficient funds by 1222 to again address itself to the question of a naval defence force for the kingdom and perhaps Hubert's influence in Ireland through his nephew's high office there was a factor. The state papers for July 1222 list the building of galleys in the eastern Irish ports 'for the king'; and a little later in August the same year, the harbourmaster at Winchelsea, Paulyn de Winchelsea, was ordered to go to nearby Rye to check on the state of some galleys delivered there.[4] As noted earlier, it is probably to Richard I's reign that the original offensive ships of the first Royal Navy can be traced, but Hubert – seen after Sandwich as demonstrating an accomplished marine knowledge – seemingly took steps to ensure the continuance of his inherited sea defence assets during his tenure as principal advisor to the young Henry III. Certainly there was at this time a senior post established in the Cinque Ports of 'Keeper of the Galleys' – vessels built specifically for offensive, not trading purposes – during the period of Hubert's control of these ports. One authority states that John had at least twenty galleys dispersed in various ports, and by the end of his reign Henry III had increased this to possibly fifty.[5] Hubert de Burgh seems likely to have held a supervisory role over the management of these types of vessels during his Cinque Ports era, namely at the two-galley dock at Winchelsea, and the seven-galley one at Rye.[6]

Margaret's influence in taking some of the stress out of Hubert in the daily exercise of his great office can be glimpsed from some accounts entries for 1222. On 22 February the castellan of Windsor Castle, Engelhard de Cigogné, was given orders to lend to Hubert the castle's dog pack so that he, together with Jordan the forester, might hunt the fox and hare in Windsor Forest. Later in the year, and almost certainly for a Hogmanay style New Year's celebration, probably at his Banstead estate, Engelhard was again called upon, this time to capture three fallow deer in Windsor Forest for the special delectation of Margaret, and to send the deer to the lady. While this was not quite in Monarch of the Glen league, it shows Margaret very quickly accumulating knowledge of what her complex and forthright husband would enjoy away from the office.

Though obviously he worked largely within the Westminster court complex, up to this point in his career only one evidential source is known to say where else Hubert stayed privately when in London: apparently he had a house south of the Thames in Southwark. Possibly this house had come to him as part of the Banstead estate; for Banstead parish church, adjacent to which Hubert's newly acquired manor house stood, had been the property of the Convent of St Mary Overie, Southwark (today Southwark Cathedral) since the reign of Henry I. In any event, it was about now (1222/1223) that he passed this Southwark property on to one Alan de Wicton, and then helped himself to a very high quality residence about halfway along the thoroughfare then called King Street but which we know today as Whitehall.[7] This Thameside mansion of William of Ely, the King's Treasurer, had come on to the market following William's death in 1222. The property was owned by the monks of Westminster Abbey and William had lived in and worked from the house for many years, but he suffered indictment of compliance with the invading force during the French occupation of London and had to forfeit his tenure and relinquish his court role of Treasurer. However, being an elderly 'sitting tenant' and unwell, the Westminster monks took a charitable view and allowed him to stay on in the house for his last years. Likewise, William's son Ralph was also allowed to retain by goodwill various adjoining properties. Hubert had been a signatory to the revised tenancy agreement of about 1219 and so perhaps had kept an eye on the estate since then. The original deeds, dateable to around 1223, conveying the property of both William and Ralph to Hubert read as follows,

> Richard, Abbot of Westminster, grants to Hubert de Burgh, Justiciar of England, all the houses and court, with a free chapel to celebrate and hear divine service for himself and his household together within the vill of Westminster which William of Ely once Treasurer of England, held of him. Hubert to render annually to the Church of St Edward 3lbs. of wax, having paid 140 silver marks.[8]
>
> Ralph, son of William once Treasurer of England, grants to Hubert de Burgh Justiciar of England all his houses and grange which he held within the two gates of the said Hubert in the vill of Westminster, namely those houses which are adjoining the court and houses of the said Hubert, which belonged to William the Treasurer, my late father, on one side of the way within the gates, and two houses and the grange which adjoin the stable of the said William my father on the other side of the road within the same gates. Hubert to render annually to the Abbot and monks of Westminster 1lb of cumin and 1lb of wax and 1d at Pentecost, he having paid 10 silver marks.[9]

An additional conveyance made at the same time seems to refer to some part of that locality which we know today as St James's Park,

> William at the Bar grants to Hubert de Burgh Justiciar of England all the land which he held of Geoffrey at the Cross which is called 'More' and which lies between the marsh of the Hospital of St James and the moor of John the Chancellor in one direction, and between the land of Adam of the Monastery and the Thames in the other direction. He also grants to the said Hubert the services of John le Taillur [a wealthy Charing Cross tailor] due for land which the said John held of him which lies between the land of Osbert Mustard and the land of the said

John which he holds in chief of Henry de Luyton save for the service to the lord of the fee Hubert to render 1d annually for all services he having paid 6 marks.[10]

Finally, Hubert rounded off this impressive property acquisition with these further transactions – Roger of Ware, son of Robert of Westminster, and Maud of Ware, sold all their land to him lying between the property of Odo the goldsmith and the land of Levota the widow for 12 marks of silver. Odo the goldsmith sold all his land lying between that of Roger of Ware and that of Robert the carpenter, stretching between the highway and the Thames for 10 marks of silver.

So Hubert, at some very competitive prices, acquired a range of highly valuable real estate. The principal mansion itself was facing on to the Thames, with ancillary adjoining utility properties running back as far as the highway with, over the road in St James, many acres of valuable farming land; also substantial housing abutting the south side of what is today Horse Guards Avenue. In today's Whitehall geography Hubert's mansion stood between the Banqueting House and the Thames. It would have had its own private river stairs and terrace, also extensive cellarage for storage. Hubert knew some of the sellers. Odo the goldsmith was Henry III's goldsmith, and a property tycoon on the side, while William of Ely had worked at the Treasury with his son Ralph. It was at this time, on 6 February 1223, that Jordan the Windsor forester received orders to permit Hubert's men to cut and cart away from the forest the timber allocated to them for the construction of 'the palace of Hubert' in London. This was clearly destined for the upgrade of his new London pied-à-terre which, apparently, very much accorded with the description '*nobile palatium*' given it by his friend Matthew Paris. What it looked like inside can be judged by the fact that in later years, soon after Hubert's death, his King Street mansion had become so magnificent that the archbishops of York purchased it as their London palace. Hubert had indeed achieved a lifetime ambition in joining the ranks of the Thameside marine millionaires he had noticed some forty years earlier as he came down the river for the first time to Westminster. At about the date Hubert moved into his all mod cons London residence his brother-in-law Alexander came down from Scotland to visit the court: no doubt Hubert and Margaret laid on a memorable house-warming. Maybe Scotland Yard's origin?

With a relatively peaceful domain starting to emerge from the progressive governing partnership of Hubert de Burgh and Archbishop Stephen Langton, commercial trading and the fortunes of merchants across the land began to enjoy a new dawn; a major impetus initiated by the duo being a radical alteration in the currency of the realm. Up to now the basic unit of coinage, the silver penny, had been divided into halfpence and quarter pence (farthings) by the actual cutting of a penny coin into either halves or quarters. The resultant small and very fiddly partial coins were for ever being lost or wrongly accounted for. Hubert and Stephen therefore ordered the production by the national mints of new coins in halfpenny and quarter penny denominations. As with many national initiatives in which Hubert had a hand, the change for the better was long-lasting. With some cosmetic alterations over the centuries, these basic coin denominations were to survive until decimalization in 1971.

Political relations for the time being were settled with the Scots, but across the Welsh border periodic forays against the English were largely held in check by the powerful border lords, such as the Earl of Chester. In 1223 however the Welsh leader Llywelyn ab Iowerth, 'Prince of North Wales', decided to try his luck with a raid across the border into Shropshire where his force took control of the castles at Kinnerley and Whittington. When after some months he still remained in Shropshire the young William Marshal (II) heading the English opposition, much as in a game of chess, took the Welsh castles at Cardigan and Carmarthen in retaliation, as well as his own regained fortress of Kilgerran. Encouraged by the compliance of the local Welsh leader Cynan ap Hywel, William Marshal continued to consolidate his gains with the acquisition of the lordship of Kidwelly and its castle. While William was seemingly unstoppable in the south, Hubert arriving in the north set in place plans to mount an attack from Bridgnorth. Llywellyn's next move was to enclose the stronghold of Builth, powerbase of the locally influential de Braose family. Hubert then took overall command of the situation, went to Gloucester where he collected and amassed a huge English feudal force, and then fell upon the Welsh at Builth. Cowed by the size and determination of Hubert's force, the Welsh leader retreated with his forces back into their mountain fastness. Hubert then moved south to Montgomery to start the construction of a new castle there to give tighter control of the southern passes into Wales. Llywelyn had had enough at this point, with the Archbishop of Canterbury also threatening to interdict the whole Welsh kingdom and so open it to papally approved invasion by anyone. At a peace conference on 8 October at Montgomery, Llywelyn formally gave up on his Shropshire raid and returned to the King the ownership of the two castles there, also he agreed to pay due reparation for the damage his raids had caused. Hubert's contribution to the recovery of royal control of the sensitive south Wales marcher lands was not lost on the King.

Control of the royal castles was to become a central political theme in England later in 1223 when a communication, apparently papal, approved the young King being now of an age (he was 16) to rule and to seal his own documents. This conclusion of his minority meant that any castles and counties held in the King's name since his accession and during his minority would now have to be given up to him. Hubert set himself as the enforcer of this highly unpopular plan, starting with Walter de Lacy being asked to surrender Hereford, castle, shire, and fiscal control. The affronted and affected castellans formed a protective and rebellious front behind de Lacy and pointed to Hubert as the instigator of the idea to Rome: they considered it his personal plan to diminish their authority, an inevitable result of the forfeiture of their tenancy of these royal castles. Hubert protested innocence and put Peter des Roches in the frame as the senior bishop in the land and so most likely to be hand-in-glove with the papal see. The Archbishop of Canterbury collected the dissidents into a gathering in London for the return of Hubert and the King from the West Country in early December. Headed by the Poitevin Peter des Roches, those castellans at risk of loss, to a man, accused Hubert as an oppressor and, as well, waster of the royal treasure. Not a man to be threatened lightly, Hubert replied in kind, further implicating the foreign bishop as agent provocateur in the troubles of both John's and Henry's reigns. In modern parlance Peter des Roches then 'lost it', threatened to finish Hubert whatever it took, and stormed from the meeting at the head of the dissidents. Stephen Langton, who had brokered the meeting, forced the two to keep apart from each other until the end of January while he tried further mediation. What he came up with was that

Hubert's until now largely unquestioned authority over national policy and, not least, the King himself, would be tempered by the conjoint witness to his decisions of two bishops, Jocelin de Wells, Bishop of Bath, and Richard le Poer, Bishop of Salisbury. Hubert expressed himself very happy with the arrangement: now any blame for contentious issues could be shared and not placed wholly at his door.

A final eruption of the 'royal castles' dispute took place at Bedford in June 1223 when William de Breaute, the castellan there, violently assaulted the King's representative, a royal judge, and closed the castle – an act of treason. His brother Falkes, asked by the King to account for William's actions at Bedford, went into hiding. Both had been on Hubert's 'hit-list' for various infractions of law and order both before and after the death of John. The Justiciar immediately laid siege to Bedford and, after some defiance, under Henry's orders executed all found within its walls including William the castellan. His brother was hunted down near the Welsh border and then sent into exile by the King to die two years later in France. Gathering that Christmas at Leicester, the residual rebel castellans received a messenger from Henry celebrating his festival at Northampton Castle requesting they attend his party there at once and so signify their peace with the young King. Backed into a corner, they could only comply and at Northampton had read to them chapter and verse about royal castle relinquishment; the King did however concede that his Justiciar must also give up some of his holdings pro rata. Archbishop Stephen Langton proceeded to mediate between the Crown and the barons and set out the terms of relinquishment and reapportionment of the castle and county ownership. Hubert had to surrender six castles – Norwich, Orford, Rochester, Canterbury, Dover and Hereford. But some of these were only on a temporary or nominal basis. Whereas the rebels' leader Falkes de Breaute gave up his six county castles, Ranulph of Chester gave up Lancashire, Shropshire, and Staffordshire, Peter des Roches Winchester, and William de Cantelupe Warwickshire and Leicestershire. These were permanent losses by them to the Crown.

Those castles that Hubert retained he claimed were his by virtue of his office as Justiciar, this proviso was nodded through by a compliant Henry. Hubert was in the ascendant over castle control across the country, the Poitevin bishop had lost face and power – for the time being. Even the nephew of des Roches, Peter de Reviaulx, was removed from his post at court: Hubert replaced him there with his own chaplain and closest friend, Luke of St Albans.

In 1224 occurred a significant event in Hubert's life when he voluntarily gave to the emergent order of Dominican Friars (the 'Black Friars') in London some land on which to build their first premises in the capital. Sited near the north-east corner of Shoe Lane in the City, the fraternity went from strength to strength, having eventually to move to the much larger and better known premises at Ludgate. Hubert was a principal benefactor to the order for the remainder of his life and was to retain close family connections with the brothers. Paradoxically, it was Peter des Roches who had inducted the order into the Kingdom in the first place in 1221 at the behest of the Vatican.[11] During the July of 1223 King Philip of France died. His heir, failed invader Louis, immediately started a tour of his inheritance to assess his chances of attacking the non-French provinces on his borders. The advantage Louis had were the massive reserves at the French Treasury accumulated by his father in the final years of his reign during which an unnatural peace had broken out across the French continent. The English administration had in contrast no liquid cash to spare: expenditure just about equalled costs in the years after Magna Charta, and the adopted terms of the Charter placed limitations on the taxation measures the government of the day could impose. Indeed as one modern authority states,

> It must be doubted if his [Henry III's] financial and military base in England was ever strong enough to support his ambitions on the Continent. By the 1220s he had about £15,000 a year with which to fight Louis VIII of France, whose income p.a. was about £65,000 in English money.[12]

In the records of these days occasional sidelights appear illustrating Hubert's private life as, on 25 November 1224, clearly in anticipation of a cold winter, a mandate was issued by his office to the barons of the Cinque Ports to 'give free passage to the ship of wine merchant Stephen de Croy, laden with wines of Hubert de Burgh, so that the wines may be landed safely at Sandwich'. On a more serious note Hubert had himself been accused by the Poitevin barons of wasting royal revenues to the detriment of the crown, but in fact the probable annual available national treasure value of some 30,000 marks could be viewed as a testament to the Justiciar's ability in creating something out of nothing.[13] But now further stringent financial measures had to be taken to counter the French King's newly emergent belligerent ambitions, and Hubert came up with an idea for improving the national debt which he discussed with Archbishop of Canterbury, Stephen Langton. Known to posterity as 'the Fifteenth', and with the backing of the archbishop, Hubert put to the Great Council on 1 February 1225 a proposal to levy a tax of one-fifteenth the assessed value of all chattels (belongings and moveables) of laymen and non-exempt clergy. It was not a new concept, for an original form had existed under King Richard in 1188 known as the 'Saladin Tithe' where it was applied at one-tenth rate to finance his plans in the Third Crusade – Hubert demonstrated a long memory. The Council of Magnates agreed to his proposal but took the opportunity to make it conditional upon an updated confirmation of the Magna Charta terms of the population's rights and liberties and, as well, the Forest Charter. The reissue of the Great and Forest Charters was effected under these terms on 11 February 1225, the barons in return agreeing to comply in recovering and paying to the Treasury 'the Fifteenth' due from their tenantry. The Charter wording had also to be suitably worded to reflect the new enactment: in the Preamble came the change that the new provisions were issued by the King's 'free and good will'. In the text body was inserted a condition that anyone not paying the fifteenth would be open to legal process to enforce payment.

So Magna Charta in its most applicable form has descended to modern times, much due to the machinations of Hubert de Burgh, working in conjunction with Stephen Langton.[14] Hubert had also, in gaining the agreement of the barons, won a vital victory of governmental authority over the incipient threat of their anarchical intentions. Henry did not wait very long to use his newly found income to finance an expedition to try and recover the provinces lost to France by his father. But rather than risk his own neck he sent instead his younger brother, Richard, Earl of Cornwall, in March 1225 with generals the Earl of Salisbury and Philip d'Aubigny. Created Count of Poitou for the expedition, Richard made a successful tour through Gascony, impelling the allegiance of the Poitevins, more with financial arm-bending than with military force. At the same time a complex programme of political negotiations was in hand with the supposed allies opposed to the French cause in the northern and eastern countries bordering France. But when push came to shove these shaky alliances were to quickly disassemble.

Hubert meanwhile had suffered a family embarrassment in the form of his hotheaded nephew, Reymond de Burgh, son of his brother Geoffrey. Sir William Longsword, Earl of Salisbury, commander of the English at Bouvines, and uncle to the King, was reported overdue on a sea voyage in 1225, and after some weeks with no news was assumed missing at sea. Hubert then asked the King to permit Reymond to approach the evidently widowed Countess Ela with a view to possible betrothal. Henry assented, but only provided that Ela was willing. So, in due course, suited and booted, the cocksure young Reymond on his best horse went calling on the countess. On arriving at the Salisburys' estate he found to his dismay that the news reports were out of date, and that the countess had been advised that her husband was safe and sound and on his way home by another route. To complete his embarrassment, Countess Ela told him off in no uncertain terms for trying it on, and even if the earl had died at sea she would never consent to marry someone of such ignoble rank. It got worse for both Hubert and Reymond on the earl's return. He complained to the King about allowing such a base fellow as Reymond ('*degenerum virum quondam!*') to make such approaches to his wife and would seek a revenge whatever it took. Hubert hastily took measures to save face with the King and to soothe the troubled earl: he invited him to a banquet, which invitation the earl accepted. An even worse outcome happened with the earl being taken ill after visiting Hubert and dying a short time later. Poisoning was inevitably suspected with Hubert's complicity, but nothing was ever proved and no charges made, but later in Hubert's life the incident was to resurface to haunt him. Not long after his very public rebuff Reymond successfully (and quietly) married Christiana, the dowager Countess Mandeville. Sir William Longsword became the first person to be buried in the new Salisbury Cathedral in 1226: his tomb in the south arcade shows him recumbent in armour, his heraldic arms azure, six lioncels rampant or. Countess Ela, meanwhile, founded Lacock Abbey in Wiltshire, and lived there as a nun. Her abbey's Foundation Charter was witnessed by Hubert, and William de Warenne. Not much altered with time, Lacock Abbey survives today.

In France during this time Louis had gone off on the Fifth Crusade and, to equal consternation and delight on either side of the Channel, died while abroad in November 1226. (English court astrologer, Master William Pierrepoint, had predicted Louis' death 'within the year'.) With the accession of the new king, Louis IX, aged just 12, all the dissident factions in and around the French court bubbled to the surface to realign their allegiances. In England Henry immediately put in hand plans for the 'reconquest of our inheritance'. But emerging from the curtained background of her private court came the enemy to all Henry's ambitions; Blanche of Castile – Louis' mother and regent. Within months she had neutralized the political opposition to the new King and forced Henry into a truce until mid-1227, resulting in the withdrawal of the English occupation forces from the province of Poitou. In England Henry attended to his domestic affairs by deciding to assume his ultimate power as King regnant and in January 1227 officially declared his minority at an end. He could now rule with sole authority. Consequently Stephen Langton relinquished his role as regent, happy to return his considerable administrative skills to a solely religious environment. (Perhaps he spent time polishing his revolutionary division – in 1204–5 – of the Bible into chapters and verses, as we see it today.) But Hubert could not make a similar concession. As royally appointed Justiciar he had to, *ex officio*, continue to be the King's deputy in any absence Henry might make from the realm. So he carried on more or less in the same role as closest advisor, as he had during the King's minority. But the purpose of a Justiciar was already becoming an anachronism. With the central Court departments now static and governing the realm from Westminster, gradually the realization took hold that no one person would be needed anymore to look after the shop while the King was absent elsewhere. Hubert was astute enough to see this writing on the wall for his role, but meanwhile he was not going to let the comforts and advantages of his sinecure which he had fought long and hard to attain be put at risk – while it continued, he wanted more ...

Chapter 12

1227–1230 A Foreboding of Disaster

That he was still held in the highest regard by Henry was exemplified in the February of 1227 when, at an elaborate ceremony at Oxford, Hubert was ennobled by the young King to the earldom of Kent. Approaching 60 years of age Hubert was accompanied by his family when the great honour was bestowed, namely, his wife, Margaret of Scotland, his 14-year-old son John (by Beatrice de Warrenne), and brothers Geoffrey and Thomas. There too by her mother's side was Hubert's infant daughter Margaret, whom they affectionately called Megotta. (Back in 1224 Hubert had made his daughter a considerable potential heiress by presenting her with the honours, i.e. income, of four of his most important lands.) The earldom of Kent dated from the days of the Conqueror when it had been held (and forfeited) by Odo of Bayeux; its significance to Hubert – who maybe prodded Henry with some self-promotion – was immense, permanently linking him in the historical record with all that county meant to his career, the heroics of Dover and Sandwich. Now his peerage put him on a par with those old landed gentry families who had always been quick to try and keep the upstart 'new money' Justiciar in his place. With the earldom came as well further extensive honours of lands and estates, notably in Essex and Suffolk, to add to those already accumulated in his rise up the courtly ladder. Later, on 11 July 1227, the new earl accompanied by Henry and his court, came to Dover to further add to Hubert's county prestige by consecrating a new chapel for the hospital of St Mary – the Maison Dieu – that Hubert had originally founded back in 1202. The chapel foundation charter attested by the King granted it a perpetual income from 'The tithe of the issues of the passage of the port of Dover'.[1] A substantial benefaction indeed. Although the young King and his mentor were yet to have many differences of opinion, some with almost fatal consequences, it is significant that later Henry continued for many years after Hubert had passed away to confer charters and incomes upon the Maison Dieu, so perpetuating the memory of a statesman to whom he was to concede a grudging, if retrospective, respect.[2] Although inevitably altered in structure and purpose over the intervening centuries, the Maison Dieu and its chapel still survive today, forming an enduring monument to Hubert de Burgh's philanthropy. Its glorious stained glass windows were added in 1873 by EJ Poynter; the image of Hubert de Burgh occupies the centre one.

In Wales Hubert had also attained great influence. In addition to his 'Three Castles', he acquired in 1228 control of Montgomeryshire, to be followed in 1229 by Cardigan and Carmarthen. But although by dint of 'conveyance at court' he had acquired the title to these vast lands which controlled the vital southern approaches to Wales, Hubert was never to gain any political supremacy with the native Welsh leaders. Perhaps these latest Welsh estates were an acquisition too far for Hubert. Ownership of them gave him added leverage with the English court, but over the border waited Llywelyn ab Iorwerth, the great Prince of the North, whose diplomatic skills maintained the various provinces of Wales under his control. He was ready for any incursion the English might attempt northwards from their southern holdings: could Hubert muster the necessary firepower to fulfil his Welsh ambitions? In respect of his 'Three Castles' in the south, a monument to Hubert's religious feelings still survives at Grosmont. It exists in the church of St Nicholas which displays its breathtaking original timber roof constructed in *c.*1227 under Hubert's direction, using fifty oaks taken from Herefordshire Trevill forest. They were gifted to him by Henry for the church's restoration. It remains the only surviving pre-1400 church roof in Wales.

With his career approaching its zenith Hubert was, by now, one of the richest men in the kingdom, his income as estimated by one authority was equivalent to more than one-tenth of the King's.[3] He could afford a wide circle of influential retainers as well as an extensive household staff which included chaplains for both himself and Margaret, personal cooks, doctors, butlers, household managers, etc. for his King Street mansion in Westminster, not to mention the many hundreds of retainers across some fourteen counties who controlled and managed the county assets he had acquired over the years. But Hubert's personal magnificence was starting to create a blind spot in his perceptions of the world he moved in; he had become habitual in thinking his wealth and influence were always going to be there, he just had to keep his eye on the ball. Maybe it was senior age complacency, rheumatic irascibility, who knows, but Hubert started to miss vital signs of change until its effects were almost upon him – and he lacked a thought-through back-up plan. A critical factor in this was Hubert's arch-enemy, Peter des Roches, Bishop of Winchester. He had been absent from England since 1227 when he had taken the crusader's cross and been in Damietta on Holy Land duty. More significantly he had been amassing good behaviour points with the Vatican as go-between for the crusade sponsor Frederick II and Pope Innocent III. In the event of his return to England, Peter des Roches would carry with him a potent European power base. Additionally Hubert was starting to outlive his contemporaries, men who had backed him and his policies in past times: William Brewer, Martin de Pateshull, William Longsword, and most significantly Stephen Langton, Archbishop of Canterbury who died in July 1228 at his Manor of Slindon in Sussex. A close friend as well as the one for whose advice Hubert always had the highest regard: Hubert attended Stephen's funeral at Canterbury Cathedral later in the month. With these supports to his position at the young King's side irrevocably vanishing, Hubert needed to watch his back. He was in danger of being overtaken by the up and coming younger radicals who, in turn, were supported by others whose families had been disaffected by Hubert's self-serving policies of earlier years. They, more and more, perceived him and particularly his office of Justiciar, as outmoded and redundant.

But the King, to Hubert's despair, was starting to show signs of growing into a typical hotheaded Angevin, high on self-esteem, short on vision, and shorter still on patience. Henry remained blind to the efforts his Justiciar expended in keeping the concerns of an English kingdom at the forefront of their plans and policies; in particular, Hubert's own successful fiscal achievements that he had pushed through with the successive Magna Charta issues. Consequently Henry now had an Exchequer with cash to spend. Also Hubert's nephew Richard could show success by a relatively quiescent Ireland; while the Scottish connection through Hubert's wife continued to keep the clans from threatening incursions south across the border. Taking this relative stability of his realm for granted, Henry started to look abroad for a means to elevate his profile both with his favourites in England, and with the continental courts. He revisited the cause of recovering the lost English provinces – Brittany, Normandy, Maine, Anjou, and Poitou. He had, after all, styled himself 'Henry by the Grace of God King of England, Lord of Ireland, Duke of Normandy and Aquitaine, and Earl of Anjou'. Temporarily distracting Henry's mind from his lofty ambitions Hubert was to take great satisfaction in seeing his son John knighted by the King on Whitsunday 1229.

Of Hubert's other relations, Richard, his nephew by his deceased elder brother William, had been appointed Justiciar of Ireland, after maintaining a relatively peaceful government there. But both Thomas and Geoffrey, his younger siblings, led lives of quiet meandering in East Anglia. Thomas, no more than a local squire, was to die in 1227 with no children from his wife Nesta, while Geoffrey viewed life from the rather more lofty perspective of Ely Cathedral to which bishopric he had been consecrated by Stephen Langton in June 1225. His brief and quiet tenure came to an equally quiet end in the winter chills of the Fens on 8 December 1228, Geoffrey being laid to rest in his Ely Cathedral with due solemnity four days later. Hubert, of course, had kept in touch with all his brothers, and was ready to make a useful pathway for any aspiration they exhibited. Likewise too, with his close friends, as Luke of St Alban's his life-long chaplain would testify, as he acceded to the Archdeaconry of Norwich left vacant by Geoffrey. Not too many years ahead Hubert would see Luke assume the Archbishopric of Dublin and he would see him join forces with Richard de Burgh to form a shrewd political partnership that would guide that sometimes insecure province further forward towards a more stable future.

During the second half of 1228 a steady stream of continental 'advisors' visited the English court, happy to indulge the inexperience of the young King who had yet to set foot outside his country and had no idea of the realities of taking on the French on their own soil. Hubert had been there and done all of that, and had the scars. Nearly 60 years of age he had absolutely no interest in once again suffering the rigours of what he knew would be a fruitless quest against haughty French barons who changed their allegiances like spinning weathervanes. And besides all that, a Vatican approved truce between England and France still remained in force until July 1229. Hubert, though still the King's principal politician, now possessed no authority to give him orders, all he could do was to tactfully remind Henry to consider these factors and to proceed with caution. The King considered instead that the intelligence he was receiving from across the Channel – which seemingly indicated a large force of friendly baronage awaiting his arrival – outweighed his Justiciar's caution and he threw himself into preparations to lead an expeditionary force to regain his father's lost inheritance. Consequently he signed the orders for a fleet, fully provisioned, to be ready to leave from Portsmouth in the October of 1228. A reluctant but ever-loyal Hubert was numbered among those required to accompany the King. However, on arriving at Portsmouth at the due time, Henry found nowhere near enough ships (a little over seventy) had been assembled for the task proposed. His initial reaction was to give Hubert a violent dressing-down in public on the quayside even, according to one source, drawing his sword and threatening Hubert's life.[4] The old Justiciar still had many friends at court though, and those present at the altercation intervened, particularly Earl Ranulf of Chester, to allow the infuriated and embarrassed Henry to regain some composure, and for Hubert to reassess his position.

There is no evidence on record that Hubert deliberately put in hand plans to sabotage the expedition, as Henry initially charged him, but clearly he was the one man in the kingdom who could bring pressure to bear on the critical logistical points of the King's plan without Henry's realization. Hubert knew all about covering his tracks. Had he been culpable, he knew too that he would be singled out by Henry on the day for blame, but what he may have misjudged was the severity of that blame. Henry had been publicly hurt in that most significant of places, his pride, and Hubert's possible involvement was not to be forgotten. Little doubt too that news of the row found its way to Peter des Roches on the continent and would help him judge the most opportune moment to return and cause Hubert the maximum discomfiture. But another factor may have caused Hubert to, for the first time, allocate his loyalty to his monarch to second place in his thinking. Hubert had been married to Margaret now for some eight years, they had a daughter they doted on, a very comfortable lifestyle with all the best that their medieval world could bring, including an opulent palace next to the King's in London, and a superb country estate at Banstead to get away from it all. It is surely certain that Margaret must have tried to influence her probably by now arthritic husband to try and opt out of the privations of what would obviously be a life-threatening journey to an alien nation that he hadn't visited for a decade and a half. We may say Margaret loved Hubert and wanted to keep him safe, she must have told him as much. Hard man though he was, the growing discomforts of old age must have cautioned him, at the very least, to listen to her heartfelt advice. At the same time, Margaret would certainly have wanted to protect and preserve her ennobled lifestyle. Henry's autumn expedition never got started, and Hubert had slipped a rung down the ladder of royal favour which he would never regain: as various commentators agree, from 1229 Henry began to rule as well as to reign: perhaps he was thinking he could now do so without the aid of his old mentor – time would soon tell.

Chapter 13

1230–1231 Henry's Odyssey of Wasted Time

The breach between Henry and Hubert was temporarily mended the following year when the King ordered his Justiciar to again assist in plans to raise an expeditionary force to cross the Channel with the intention of recovering the lost provinces. It seemed that Hubert was still the one man in Henry's life powerful enough to influence his thinking. Henry's intelligence appeared to suggest that the coalition supporting the dominant forces of Blanche of Castile would disintegrate if an English army pushed hard enough in the right places. There were certainly many intertwined interests between the barons in England, both Angevin and British, and their equivalents, the numerous counts vying for power in Brittany, Normandy, Anjou, and Poitou.

An essential initial measure was to bring to the south coast a shipping fleet large enough for the task, one far greater than that which had enraged Henry at Portsmouth. So in November 1229 all the sheriffs of counties having major ports were ordered to commandeer any ships in their harbours large enough to carry a minimum of sixteen horses. Additionally, any ships of similar size arriving at these ports between November and the following Easter were also to be impounded into the King's service. This measure was not royal piracy, for the King paid the ship's masters for the enforced hire of their vessels. Nor were these belligerent naval ships, but heavy duty cargo ships which, in their normal usage, carried anything for anyone to anywhere. But it was also just one element of the eventually huge expenditure which, to Hubert, was a pointless waste of the Exchequer funds that he had so carefully helped to amass for Henry since the end of John's reign. Hubert's intentions were always that the English population should reap the eventual benefits of the fiscal policies that both he and Langton had championed: that this cash should now be poured into a bottomless pit of Angevin ambition was an anathema to him. Even Hubert's brother-in-law, Alexander of Scotland, was persuaded to chip in with a 2,000 marks donation. He had come down to York for a family Christmas with Henry, only to leave less well off than he came. Between a rock and a hard place, Hubert for now had to play along and indeed go along, literally, with the King on his futile escapade. He had at least done his best by counselling Henry to open his campaign in the south where Henry's mother Isabella and her husband, Hugh de Lusignan, held sway.

By mid–April 1230 all was ready again at Portsmouth. Massed around the harbour were about 450 requisitioned vessels, from these the most seaworthy 300 were selected to make the voyage across the Channel. The remainder, being released from further obligation, sailed off. The army numbering possibly 5,000 was assembled under the leadership of nine earls, including Hubert, and about 400 knights.[1] Hubert's own contingent numbered some four knights – Henry de Muneghdon, Thomas de Bavelingham, Philip de Perry and Robert Fitznicholas. Other of Hubert's nobility pressed into service included John and Ranulph Brito, Gilbert de Bosco, Robert Aguillun, and Richard Alencon. Hubert's son John and his nephew Reymond also had their complement of knights. One thing his boys would be watching was the chest containing Hubert's travelling cash, about 1,400 marks (hundreds of thousands today). Back home Hubert had arranged for Margaret, together with Megotta to live in safety at any royal castle that she wished for the duration of his absence. The King didn't stint himself either, according to the records taking eight chests of jewellery, a new wardrobe of state clothing, his royal cup and basin, but then only his second-best ruby ring.

By the end of the month the loading was complete and on 1 May the King's ill-considered adventure started. A couple of days later the landing was made at St Malo, ignoring Hubert's advice to make a landfall in the south. With Hubert near at hand Henry led his force on to Nantes having hoped to meet his mother Isabella and her husband Hugh de Lusignan. They failed to appear at the appointed time and place leaving Henry undecided about the prospects of what local support, if any, he might count on. Six weeks later he and the army were still there, the inactivity breeding fights and drunken quarrels between the soldiery and the unfortunate locals. All the while the French force controlled by Blanche of Castile had been shadowing the English from a distance. Unbeknown to Henry at the time

Blanche held the trump card of a recently agreed non-aggression pact with the Lusignan family who controlled the great province of Poitou, and that was why Isabella and Hugh had kept clear of Henry's invasion. They too saw no purpose in his ambition, preferring to keep the peace with their French neighbours which, of course, meant the lesser families falling into line behind the all-powerful Lusignan faction. After a couple of sabre-rattling forays along the Loire valley to forestall local defection to Henry, Blanche and her army returned to Paris, leaving Henry still static and wondering what to do next. Hubert's exact counsel to Henry at this time remains unrecorded but he knew certainly that the relatively small English force could neither defeat the French with their huge reserves of manpower and ready cash, nor could it successfully assault any of the strategically important royal castles. So possibly he steered Henry towards more of a flag-waving tour through the lost provinces just to let him see what he was up against: this was after all the King's first trip across the Channel and the thought was not lost on Hubert that he had a responsibility to get the young man back safely to England afterwards. His job (and life) depended on it. And this, more or less, was the course of events that ensued, with Henry and his host trudging south and west, occasionally knocking over a relatively unimportant fortress more for morale than for achievement. Hubert was probably happiest when they got down to Bordeaux in early August. There he could get out of the saddle, look up his friends from his old days there as Seneschal of Poitou, listen to the news, and get decent bed and board. It had been fifteen years since he last enjoyed the continental version of good wine, good food, and warm spring sunshine: he had much to catch up on.

As he progressed across the old domains there were certain barons unhappy with the French who approached Henry for backing, but he could offer little of substance, and certainly no agreements of any longevity. So far as Henry was concerned it was 'don't call us, we'll call you'. The expedition was fated to fail in every way, even to many of the force contracting a virulent illness just before embarking for home, resulting in the death of several of the most elderly earls, and even Henry himself being confined to bed and not able to return when planned. But when on 26 October the King did set sail for home, Hubert could at least say he had got Henry back in one piece, though later the ungrateful monarch would try and charge his Justiciar with a policy of over-caution which compromised the expedition's strategy. It says much too of Hubert's political accomplishments in the recent decades that both he and the King could leave the country for an open-ended trip abroad without any unlawful uprising breaking out in their absence. Left to govern the country had been Chancellor Ralph Neville, Bishop of Chichester, and Stephen de Segrave, as Justiciar. Their joint authority was confined to their only having Hubert's official seal under which to issue any necessary writs: Henry had taken his royal great seal with him, a clear demonstration of Hubert's still viceroyal power. Some historians have berated Hubert as vacillating and not supporting the King during this campaign. Hubert wasn't a 'make your mind up' man, but instead knew from hard and painful experience when to advise his recalcitrant and mercurial monarch and, much more importantly, when not to. Far different yardsticks of survival from today were applicable 800 years ago. Sadly, in the pointless expedition Hubert had suffered a family bereavement in the death of his extrovert young nephew Reymond. Clad in full mail, Reymond had fallen into the deep, swift waters of the Loire and drowned when his horse lost its footing on the river bank. Hubert had helped in the recovery of the body of a much-loved nephew and then accompanied the coffin back to England that October for eventual interment in his Maison Dieu hospital at Dover. A measure of Hubert's depth of feeling against the King about his loss of Reymond on this totally useless expedition can be gauged from the memorial he coerced Henry to grant. It took the form of an immediate charter to the hospital of '50s yearly from the issues of the port for the support of a chaplain celebrating divine service daily in the hospital for the soul of Reymund de Burge'.[2] That added up to a fair sum of money.

Back home and reunited with his family, Hubert picked up where he had left off. The rigours of the last months decided him to accumulate further rich pickings for his old age, so he negotiated with the King to purchase the custody of the widespread lands of the late Earl of Hertford and Gloucester, Gilbert de Clare. The earl had been one of those struck down by disease in Brittany in October 1230; by the end of November Hubert had acquired his properties which stretched across half the counties in the land. Barely waiting for the King's formal permission, he purchased also the custodies of the lands of other deceased expedition members, ultimately making him, after the King, probably the greatest landowner in the realm.[3] The rightful heir to the great de Clare estates was the 8-year-old Richard de Clare, but not being of an age to assume legal control of his inheritance, Hubert applied for and was granted his eminently lucrative wardship. In these months Hubert could have invented the phrase 'don't get mad, get even!' as he made Henry pay for the humiliation at Portsmouth, the physical demands on Hubert of the pointless invasion, and his nephew Reymond's untimely and unnecessary death. Choking back his sorrow and sheathing his vindictiveness, Hubert then put on his best bib and tucker to end the year 1230 on a more positive note by crossing the Thames to Archbishop of Canterbury Richard le Grante's Lambeth Palace to join the Christmas festivity of King and court.

At this period, the early 1230s, Hubert had reached the peak of his property acquisitions – he had become a real estate legend in his own lifetime – though his acquisitions often ran ahead of his income. The following summary is what the King allowed him to own at that time, most being 'gifts', which he had accepted as a favour owed to him by the donor:

- Hatfield Peveril (Essex) the gift of William de Mandeville.
- Burgh, Sotherton, Beeston, Newton (Norfolk and Suffolk).
- Wormegay, Stowe, North Runcton, Finborough (Norfolk and Suffolk), Harthill (Yorks.), Fletching (Sussex), Portslade, (Sussex), the lands of his wife Beatrice.
- Apsley Guise and Henlow (Bucks. and Beds.), the gift of Rainald de St Valerie.
- Ringstead, Chelveston, and Stanwick (Northants.), the gift of the Earl of Ferrers.
- Wheatley (Notts.), the gift of the Countess of Eu.
- Elmore (Gloucs.), the gift of Roger fitzNicholas.
- Minsterworth (Gloucs.), leased from Henry de Minsterworth.
- Winford (Dorset), the gift of Gilbert de l'Aigle.
- Banstead (Surrey), the gift of William de Mowbray.
- Sheen (Surrey), from William de Colville.
- Tunstall (Kent), the gift of Robert de Arsic.

- Lands in Newington, Ackholt, and Roseland, Kent, the gift of the Count of Guines.
- Kingsdown (Kent), the gift of Rainald of Cornhill.
- Compton, (Warwickshire), the gift of Matilda, Countess of Essex.
- Walewood, (Warwickshire), the gift of Thomas of Walewood.
- Houses in Westminster.

The acreage of all these properties is impossible now to ascertain, but must have been vast, and Hubert either wholly owned, or had income from all of them. Nor does the above include the de Clare acquisitions. The 'houses in Westminster' Hubert transferred into a trust deed at about this time, to keep his hugely valuable London estate from Henry's grasp. The Trustees were Walter of St Martin's, minister of the Cross of Christ; Laurence of St Alban's, rector of the church of Attlebury; and Richard of Wokindon, rector of the church of Anvillers.

While in France, and against Hubert's strongest advice, Henry had sent messengers to the Vatican requesting a new papal legate be sent to England. As noted earlier, the responsibilities of the previous one had been assumed by Archbishop Langton, as senior churchman of the land. There had been no objection to that arrangement then, so why change it now? After considerable persuasive argument with the arrogant young Henry, Hubert's political arguments prevailed and the messengers were recalled. But the problem was only postponed. In the New Year Hubert and Archbishop Le Grante were to oppose each other in a dispute concerning the ownership of Tonbridge Castle. Formerly part of the Earl of Gloucester's lands, the castle had been granted by Henry to Hubert when he purchased its custody on the earl's death. But the archbishop now claimed that the earl's holding was by honour of the see of Canterbury, and the castle was theirs, and could they have it back, please? Hubert declined and Henry sat on the fence, so le Grante took his case to Rome. Once there the castle issue took a back seat as le Grante proceeded to vilify Hubert to the papal court with the charges that he alone constantly advised the King, ignoring any input both from other senior peers and as well senior church officials from le Grante downwards. Hubert also, he said, offered preferments to English bishops and clergy as opposed to those of Angevin or Italian origin. But the row expired like a blown out candle when Archbishop le Grante expired likewise on the way home that August. The papal court closed the file, allowing Hubert to continue his personal policy of trying to maintain a majority proportion of Englishmen in the English governing body.

At about this time Hubert completed for himself the construction of Hadleigh Castle in south Essex.[4] It was intended to be a kind of early warning site for the protection of his homeland assets in East Anglia. Visiting the impressive remains which still stand there today, one can see the skill which Hubert brought to its siting. Standing high on an isolated promontory on the north riverbank, the castle commands a view towards the North Sea as far east as Southend, and as far west as the Isle of Dogs. Nothing could have been landed in the Thames Estuary anywhere near Hadleigh Castle without the defenders having ample time to counter the threat. Artist John Constable made several evocative depictions of the ruins in the 1820s; his original finished work – of which he was very proud – resides in the Yale Centre for British Art, Connecticut.

During 1231 Hubert again had cause to subdue threatening raids on his great south Wales domains. By now, through his continuous property acquisitions, particularly those of his new wardship of the Clare heir, he had control of virtually all the counties from Hereford west to the Gower peninsula, and the native Welsh saw him as a considerable threat to their claims for autonomy from the English crown. Showing his nature as a quite ruthless, determined antagonist, Hubert had the leaders of the force that stormed his castle at Montgomery beheaded, sending the heads to Henry to show he had the situation under control. The arrival of that gruesome, maggot-infested consignment at Westminster can be imagined. The local citizens along King Street recoiling from the reeking, blood dripping cart; Henry taking one stomach-churning glance inside before violently retching: on recovering he ordered the contents to be tipped into the Thames at the next high water. He must have wondered about his Justiciar's methods of a Welsh final solution on this occasion. But Hubert got the Welsh question wrong, as Llywelyn proved when, learning of Hubert's display of 'justice', he promptly declared all out war on the British, marching his men to guerrilla assaults on castle after castle up and down the English border and throughout Hubert's southern strongholds. Hubert's castellan skills advised his next move. He discussed the potential threat to national security with Henry and encouraged the King to think that English authority in Wales could actually be extended if a counter-attacking army could push the Welsh back and then a new line of defensive castles built further into the native hinterland. Henry was persuaded by Hubert's argument and a large British force led by them both fought the Welsh back to their mountains during the July of 1231. Hubert then rebuilt Montgomery and, further up the Wye Valley in Powys, pulled down the old Norman motte-and-bailey at Painscastle replacing it with a permanent stone structure. Significant remains of his work survive there to the present day. However, one contemporary observed that 'while the king restored Painscastle, Llywelyn in the march of Wales destroyed ten'.

Chapter 14

1232–1234 Fortitude and Survival

Chroniclers of Hubert de Burgh's contribution to English state affairs, even to the present day, have habitually described this period of his life as being his 'disgrace', his 'fall', his 'demise'.[1] It is unambiguously documented that he was elbowed from his power base by the rapacious Poitevin faction that formed itself around the vacillating Henry, but certainly no disgrace was attached to the expedients to which Hubert was driven to keep one step ahead of the Poitevin plotters. Yes, to survive he was forced to surrender much of his privileges and property but, by shrewd political footwork; he also regained most of them. After their brief honeymoon of power at Court these same Poitevins were driven from influence, never to return. Hubert lived to fight another day, and did return. Far from the attack on his person and character being his 'demise', 'disgrace', or 'fall', he was still too clever a political animal for Henry to outwit: his literacy and legal lucidity rebutted all that the King could throw at him. In the end Henry was to give up and leave him in peace.

It was while Henry was still at Painscastle during the July of 1231 that the conspiracy theory to lever Hubert away from the King began to surface. A deputation of Poitevin adherents arrived there ostensibly on a goodwill visit to Henry consisting of Peter des Roches, Peter de Mauley, William de Cantiloupe, Earl Ranulph of Chester, Count Peter de Dreux of Brittany, Richard Marshal younger brother of the late, great William, and Simon de Montfort. Also in the background was Peter de Rievaulx, nephew of Peter des Roches. As Count of Brittany, Peter de Dreux had long been a continuous drain on the English finances, Henry constantly paying him off as a political ally to try and keep his foot in the door to the lost provinces. Hubert had for some time been trying to wean Henry away from the Brittany mirage by suggesting the advantages to the home kingdom that could accrue if Henry considered marriage to the younger sister of Hubert's Scottish wife

Margaret. However, the continental clique was keen to promote its opposing plan for Henry to consider Count Peter's daughter, Yolande of Brittany, as a partner. Once again the facile King opted for the continental dream and disregarded Hubert's advice. But when Earl Ranulph tried also to tell Henry to give Llywelyn a free hand in Wales, the King, already in the midst of fortifying his front line, deferred to an outraged Hubert and sent Ranulph away.

Meanwhile another factor came to the boil at just this time to muddy the waters even more for Hubert. An English clandestine movement had for some time been opposing the papal policy of appointing Italian clergy (many of whom never left Italy) to benefices in England to the financial detriment of the indigenous clergy. As an example, in the diocese of Lincoln alone at this time some forty benefices were held there in the name of 'foreigners'. The imposition was in part an inheritance from John's reign where he had granted 'pensions' to favoured papal envoys to keep in favour with Rome and, although disputing that these provisions belonged to another reign, Henry continued to grant the payments to selected incumbents. At least twelve cardinals across Europe also received financial 'aid' from the English Exchequer solely for the benefit of their families. The system was self-perpetuating as those 'foreigner' incumbents actually residing in England could advise the Vatican well in advance when particularly choice benefices were to become vacant enabling the Pope to specifically request that these be filled by his nominees. Apparently starting in Kent but quickly spreading across the country, growing numbers of instances were being recorded of the property of these 'foreigner' clergy being stolen, and their grain and food stores redistributed to the poor. Even papal messengers were not safe, at least one being ambushed and killed. Hubert, as Earl of Kent, received a mandate to order the arrest of those involved in the attacks in that county, but little effect was observed. Nor were the English laymen alone in their opposition, the majority of the English clergy turned a blind eye too. This continuing under-swell of antipathy to papal control in the affairs of England and foreigners generally in the country trying to direct the lives of the native English, might be distantly likened to the English anti-American feeling in the 1940s, also mostly evident in East Anglia and the south-east, that they were 'over here, over paid ...', etc. Certainly both the growing Poitevin influence combined with the strengthening assertion of papal dictates requiring the native English to fall into line behind Rome was becoming a countrywide irritant. As is apparent from his contemporary account of the times, the foremost chronicler, Matthew Paris, held these 'aliens' and as well the Poitevin ruling class, in the greatest contempt, noting that they enjoyed more land ownership and corresponding social status in England than they ever did in France. The Bishop of London, Roger Niger, took the lead in the re-imposition of law and order concerning implanted papal clergy in England, and the government eventually decided to intervene and arrest the apparent leader of the anti-papacy movement, a young knight, Sir Robert Tweng from Yorkshire. He received no more than a slap on the wrist, which further enraged the papal court on receipt of the news.[2] The next move of Pope Gregory was destined to take Hubert to the edge of a slippery slope and to recover from which danger would require all his accumulated skills of survival and resilience. Gregory appointed commissioners to carry out a papal investigation into the 'foreigner' attacks and report the findings to himself and the King. The commissioner leading the inquiry was to be the papally favoured Peter des Roches – Hubert could not win.

By the spring of 1232 Hubert had made it onto the Vatican's list as public enemy number one. Their case was that as Justiciar he should have taken the disciplinary lead from the outset, but instead had made it obvious that he felt his national people had right rather than the Vatican on their side. Henry, ever the compliant papal puppet, took the view that Hubert could and should have done more, and sooner. With this growing anti-Hubert impetus the Poitevins now moved to further unsettle him. At a council of magnates loaded with their followers in March 1232, the vote for more money to subdue possible Welsh insurrection, as recommended by Hubert, was defeated in favour of financing the Poitevin policy of the pursuit of recovering lands in Brittany. To add to Hubert's discomfort the Welsh Prince Llywelyn (probably incited by Earl Ranulph of Chester) now reassumed his offensive against the royal forces. Henry could not now finance sufficient English forces to oppose him, the majority of Henry's government having voted for the Brittany option. The Poitevins twisted the knife by being quick to point out that the blame for the King's apparent Exchequer poverty should be laid at the door of his Justiciar whose policies he had been following. That Henry liked to spend his tax income as fast as he received it was not discussed: whatever Hubert's fiscal measures had been able to raise for his King subsequent to Magna Charta (quite a substantial sum) Henry had found an expendable purpose for. But Henry had now figuratively locked arms with the cross-channel clique: everything they told him about Hubert he chose to believe. Virtually without documentary agreement Peter des Roches started to push those of his closest circle into court posts that Hubert had taken care to keep primarily in English hands. Peter des Roches's nephew Peter des Rievaulx came in for early preferment collecting in June the Treasurership of the Chamber, followed soon by custody of the Mint, then the ports and exchanges of the realm: the Poitevin counter-attack on Hubert's influence looked like becoming unstoppable. Hubert meanwhile, in retaliation, got himself appointed Justiciar of Ireland for life, with his nephew Richard his deputy there: perhaps he had visions of it being a future bolthole.

There then followed a strange, indeed unique, moment in Hubert's fortunes when the King, wishing to visit the holy site at Bromholm on the Norfolk coast, was persuaded by Hubert to enjoy the hospitality of his nearby Burgh estate.[3] The Rood of Bromholm was an obscure Cluniac Priory which claimed to have come into the possession of relics of the Holy Cross. The ecclesiastic Henry was converted to the belief on his first visit in 1226 that their relic was original and granted the monks a weekly market and an annual fair of three days on the festival of the Holy Cross (13–15 September). Henry willingly dined under Hubert's roof on 1 July 1232 (happy as ever to enjoy the benefits of other people's hard-earned money) and, while under his Justiciar's roof, seemingly set out a charter, first to Hubert's wife Margaret of an oath to the effect that 'the king has made oath on the gospels … that he will faithfully, without fraud or guile … observe all the charters which he has granted to Margaret, countess of Kent … so that neither he nor his heirs shall in any way contravene them …' and secondly in favour of Hubert 'Notification that H. de Burgh, Earl of Kent, justiciar of England, has made oath by the king's order that, if ever the king of his free will or at the suggestion of any should desire to invalidate the charters gifts, grants and confirmations made to the said H. de Burgh and Margaret his wife … the said Hubert will take care to impede that purpose, and do all in his power to preserve the said charters inviolate.' The original documents exist today on the Calendar of Charter Rolls, i 164–5, 2 July 1232.

What prompted Henry to make this sworn demonstration of fidelity to Hubert and Margaret remains unclear – why now, why there? And whose idea was it? It had one clear consequence though, it almost wrong-footed Hubert. Before the end of the month Henry's real meaning became apparent when the King appointed Poitevin Peter de Rievaulx on 28 July to take control of the government of Ireland. Hubert's role was now neutralized both in the English and Irish governments. The final stroke by the embittered Poitevin clique came the following week when, prompted by them, the King demanded from Hubert a full accounting of the expenses of his Justiciarship since Magna Charta in 1215 – and to be submitted in six weeks, please!

Hubert's lifelong survival instincts now kicked in. The Poitevins had smeared his character to the King, inaccurately but effectively, and now, aged nearly 65, Hubert could look to few contemporary friends for help, he had outlived most of them. He would have to go it alone as, without doubt, the next demand would be for his life. He kept the Bromholm Charter incident in the back of his mind for future reference, but then set himself for an episode not paralleled in the life of any other senior English statesman before or since. Hubert would be physically chased like a hunted animal by his King across the counties of the realm he had done so much to protect from mortal dangers both at home and from abroad. So while Henry's attention was diverted in transferring in August everything of Hubert's castles and lands that he could to the principal Poitevin courtiers, Peter des Roches, Peter de Rievaulx and Peter de Rivallis – now his chief advisors – Hubert got himself out of town. He went to the sanctuary of Merton Priory, some five miles north of his Banstead estate where the Prior, Henry de Basinges, welcomed him. In these times 'Sanctuary' was achieved when those seeking it could touch the ring of the knocker on the sanctuary porch door. The 'Sanctuary' thus gained (from the pursuers) was held to be valid for thirty-seven days under ecclesiastical law of the time. (Holy Trinity Church at Stratford-upon-Avon still has its original sanctuary knocker dating from the 1200s.)

Hubert had gained some time to prepare his escape plan in more detail. He knew that Henry was at his weakest when faced by any ecclesiastical authority, from papal down to parochial; if he could keep himself within the precincts of some kind of religious community then he had the best chance of survival. (Henry regularly attended two Masses a day, three times at the great feasts of Easter and Christmas.) Within the English religious community Hubert had a sympathetic following who had agreed with his policy of non-compliance on the question of the imposed Italian clergy. Interestingly, Henry's transfer of the custody of Dover Castle that September to the Poitevins was immediately strongly opposed by the Earl of Chester and the Earl of Pembroke. Already a ground swell against Henry's treatment of his long-time minister was making itself felt. A wholly foreign administration was, seemingly, not an attractive prospect for all at the King's court: some now held their cards very close to their chests. Everything that had gone wrong for Henry in his reign was now indicted against Hubert. From the campaign failure of 1230, to acting in support of the Welsh against the King, seduction of his wife Margaret prior to marriage, poisoning Archbishop le Grante on his return from Rome, there was no fantasy the King's new court failed to invent. Hubert could only for the present watch and wait at Merton for Henry's next move.

In the meantime, before he had gone to Merton, Hubert had taken prior care of Margaret sending her with Megotta away to the relative safety of Bury St Edmund's in Hubert's East Anglian homelands. With them also went his royal ward, the young 10-year-old Richard de Clare, heir to the earldom of Gloucester. Margaret, expecting the worst, made a risky decision at this time. During their virtual 'house arrest' at Bury, while Hubert was on the run, Margaret allowed a betrothal to occur between Megotta and Richard. Or, in modern parlance, she allowed them to 'sleep together'. By this means she hoped her enforced match of the two youngsters (she knew it was not a legal marriage, which would have required the King's prior consent) would result in her retention of some, if not all, of the hugely rich de Clare inheritance. Hubert was not informed of this arrangement, or so he always claimed later. Such a 'betrothal' would have effectively disqualified Richard from any marriage plans the King may have had for him after his official wardship with Hubert had expired. In fact, what was to happen was that the King used Hubert's evident outlawry to remove Richard from Bury and place him, at least temporarily, under the supervision of the Bishop of

Winchester. Later, when the full details of the events at Bury were 'leaked' to the King, he would use Margaret's complicity to further try to compound her husband's humiliation.

The King's imposed six-week wait for Hubert's defence against the trumped up charges expired about mid-September. Hubert stayed where he was; he knew that any such concocted hearing would never find in his favour. But Hubert had one friend, his old chaplain Luke who had come over from his Irish archbishopric to help his onetime master and it was Luke who would keep Hubert informed of events outside his hiding places. Non-compliance of the King's order to come to court led to Henry issuing an order for Hubert's arrest. Publication of this order incited the hooligan element of the London citizenry to form themselves into a posse and start out for Merton to take Hubert, dead or alive, on what they believed were the King's orders, and also to revenge Hubert's execution of their leaders after the 1222 riot in the capital. Peter des Roches, when consulted, made no attempt to dissuade the mob from its lynching objective. However, the more level-headed of the King's ministers saw a genie about to escape from the bottle with no hope of its return if the mob took the law into its own hands. Their wiser counsels prevailed, specifically those of Earl Ranulf of Chester, and the mob was dispersed; indeed Hubert was granted an extension of the term to account to the King until the middle of January 1233. Also the King allowed him a safe-conduct to leave Merton and go to join his family in Bury St Edmunds. Taking the King at his word in this situation was something a younger Hubert would never have done, but which the older man decided to take the risk on. Accordingly, about 24 September, he left Merton Priory to head to East Anglia. One authority states that by the first night he had reached Brentwood in Essex. The only way he could have made that mileage in that time would be if he had ridden due north from Merton a few miles to where Putney is today and then taken a boat down the Thames on the tide to somewhere near where Tilbury is today, then landed and ridden north to reach Brentwood. In this medieval time the Thames was only bridged at London, and Hubert would never risk any road route into the capital taking him close to the Tower. The only other crossings were fords well to the west of Putney which would mean a long subsequent ride of at least a couple of days from west to east through the thick woods north of the capital.

At Brentwood his worst fears were realized when he learned that Henry had sent an arrest party in pursuit of him. Evidently the King had been told by the two Poitevin Peters that Hubert's intention in escaping to his home county was to raise his adherents there in a rebellion against the King, which was a fantasy, of course, that Henry chose to believe. Taking refuge in Brentwood parish church, Hubert thought himself safe under the law of sanctuary. But the posse leader, Godfrey de Crowcumbe, had other ideas. He smashed down the church door, dragged Hubert out half-naked from the sanctuary of the church's altar, tied him to a horse, and set off back to the Tower of London, where he was thrown into a cell. Hubert's chronicler Matthew Paris suggests that the following event also took place during Hubert's arrest by the King's men and, though other contemporaries appear not to have noted it, it was to have a later resonance. Apparently, the soldiers, wishing to restrain the captive, ordered a local blacksmith to find fetters for the purpose. The smith refused, giving as his reason,

> Do to me what you please, God protect my soul for the Lord liveth, never will I put iron fetters upon him; sooner would I die. Is not he that most faithful and noble Hubert who saved all England from the invasion of the aliens and restored England to the English? Is it not he who served his lord, King John, in Gascony, Normandy, and other places so loyally and faithfully that he even had to eat horse-flesh; so faithfully that our enemies praised his remarkable constancy? Is it not he who preserved for us Dover, the key to England, against the prolonged siege of the King of France and a picked force? Who preserved our safety by defeating our enemies on the sea? God judge between him and you who treat him with such injustice and inhumanity, returning evil for good, even the worst for the best.

Hubert apparently rejoined with, 'I confess to you, Father of heaven and earth, that you have hidden my cause from the wise and mighty and have revealed it to the humble and poor. To you, my God, I reveal my cause. For my enemies raise up false witnesses against me, and evil things are spoken by them.'

But Hubert in a cell was to prove more dangerous than Hubert at large, as Henry found to his cost the next day when a fulminating Bishop of London, Roger Niger, accompanied by Archbishop Luke, berated the cowering King for gross violation of sanctuary. He demanded Hubert's return to Brentwood church immediately. So on 27 September the bishop himself collected Hubert from the Tower and took him back to Brentwood church. Within his refuge Hubert made himself comfortable, helped by two of his personal aides, for what seemed a long wait as Henry had the church surrounded with the local militia. Two weeks passed, during which time Hubert's Archbishop Luke of Dublin acted as intermediary between the hunted and the hunter. Both Hubert and Luke were playing the system, they knew the called-up guard outside was only liable for forty days' feudal service to their lords, on the expiry of that term they could just go home. To increase his hardship, on 18 October the King withdrew the concession of allowing Hubert's servants to attend him in the church, and a week later reduced his daily rations to 'a half-penny worth of bread and one great cup of beer', and his psalter was confiscated. It seems that by now most of the country had heard of Hubert's tribulations and sides were being taken for and against the old Justiciar: those for him reached Henry in a far louder voice than did those against. This feeling also found its way back to Hubert in Brentwood. With the knowledge that he still commanded a respectful backing in the country, added to which the news that his wife Margaret had enlisted the aid of the papal court in condemning the way the King had treated his first minister, he and Luke felt they were better equipped politically to counter the King's actions. So when Henry made his next move, offering Hubert the choice of being declared an outlaw or submitting to the King's will, Hubert felt on safer ground accepting the latter option.

Once more with the faithful Luke nearby, he left Brentwood to stay again in the Tower of London overnight before appearing at the King's court in Cornhill, London, on 11 November. The 'court' comprised four earls, the new Justiciar, Stephen de Segrave, and seven King's Bench judges. His wife Margaret was also there having been given a safe-conduct pass for the event. But because Hubert had already accepted the option of 'the king's mercy' there were no trial proceedings as such, only a reading of Hubert's supposed crimes (as earlier described) against the crown. Following this the King's decision was read out which shows how Henry had been influenced by the pro–Hubert following, its opening passage being,

> The king moved by pity, at the instance of the magnates of England, and at the petition of Hubert and his relatives and friends, and with the permission of the complainants, respited the judgement, ... and of free will granted the following provisions.[4]

These latter were the forfeiture of Hubert's valuables and treasure held with the Knights Templar in London (they also mortgaged his Banstead estate as security), and his renouncement of all royal lands he had acquired. He would be imprisoned in Devizes Castle, and his detention there guaranteed by the Earls of Warrenne, Pembroke, Cornwall and Lincoln, until released by the King, or if he should become a Templar and go on a crusade. The latter was not a likely option, given Hubert's advanced age. The King further agreed this would be the limitation of his punishments. Hubert had lost a lot of worldly goods, but by his character assessment of Henry he had also saved his own life by knowing when to run and when not to.

In November 1232 he started his sojourn at Devizes Castle. Why the relatively modest Devizes with all the other great fortresses to choose from? Perhaps because Henry, as a boy of 9, was himself kept secure there on his accession after his father's death in 1216 during the French invasion until after the Battle of Sandwich: it clearly had some token meaning of security to his strange mind. But, Matthew Paris noted, the chief agent of Falkes de Bréauté, Ralph de Bray, was sent to Devizes to command Hubert's guard. For the next six months Hubert led a cloistered existence at Devizes where, according to one authority, 'he ruminated on the Psalms of David in the Psalter he had with him for comfort',[5] but through the occasional visiting friend he was kept aware of any changes which might affect his security. By this means, in the September of 1233 he knew that the commanders of the castle guard had been changed from the English barony to men in the pay of the Poitevins. This could be interpreted only one way, a probable attempt on his life. Outside in the country the Poitevin faction was fast losing favour, the much promised fiscal measures to provide the King with a vast new income had not materialized, and the anti-Poitevin movement was gathering pace in the form of sporadic rebellions across the country. These outbreaks only needed a figurehead to rally behind and who better than their great hero held, they knew illegally, in Devizes. Now, feeling his years, the hardship of Hubert's captivity had recently been further increased with his being forced to wear manacles, an escape plot being suspected by his enemies. The cold and damp of his prison must also have exacerbated his suffering with agonizing rheumatism and arthritis from his old wounds. However, the stoic Hubert had found among the local garrison forming his guard several sympathetic to his cause. So, on 29 September 1233, after ensuring the night guards were at their least watchful, Hubert was helped to safety past the somnolent sentries by several of his sympathizers. Once clear of the castle precincts they all hastened to the sanctuary of the Devizes parish church of St John's.

What followed was a re-run of Brentwood, with the castle garrison eventually running the fugitives down, hauling them from the sanctuary and locking them up again in the castle cells. But again, as in East Anglia, the senior church clerics rallied to Hubert's cause in the form of Robert Bingham, Bishop of Salisbury, within whose diocese Devizes lay. Finding the castle garrison impervious to his demand to return Hubert to sanctuary, Bishop Bingham enlisted the help of Bishop of London Roger Niger, who had been Hubert's saviour in Brentwood. The pair, accompanied by their impressive clerical entourage, went to face down Henry in south Wales and demand Hubert's return to the Devizes church sanctuary. By 18 October Henry's climb-down order had been received in Devizes and Hubert was once again released to the sanctuary of the local parish church of St John's. Here he remained effectively under house arrest until the end of October. By then the guard around the church was coming to the end of its contractual feudal levy period and its manpower accordingly started to diminish by the day. At the same time the Poitevin interests in much of southern England and the Thames Valley were being raided by the growing rebel forces led by Richard Seward of Headington, and his uncle, Gilbert Basset of High Wycombe, both former comrades in arms of Hubert from Sandwich days. One initiating factor had been Henry taking Upavon Manor in Wiltshire from Gilbert Bassett to give to Peter de Mauley, Peter des Roches' closest ally, so illegally contravening a royal charter of 1229 making the manor

Bassett's in hereditary right. Other legal landowners were similarly illegally dispossessed during 1233, their royal charter rights ignored by the rapacious Poitevins.

During 28 October the depleted guard around the parish church was totally overwhelmed by a strike force of Seward's and Basset's men who had come to rescue Hubert and his servants from captivity, taking advantage of the Devizes Market Day crowds. Neutralizing the opposition, Seward's rebels freed the captives, mounted them on horseback, and set off north under cover of an opportune heavy fog to the safety of the Marshals' castle at Strigiul (Chepstow). The party crossed Severn near Ault on a boat provided by the young Earl of Pembroke and by 30 October were safely behind Chepstow's massive castle walls. Hubert had survived the Poitevin threat to his life. Now, after nearly a year of vindictive attacks upon his person and his integrity, he could recuperate and take stock of his next move.

His enforced escape from Devizes made him an outlaw in the legal terms of the day: involuntary though his abduction had been, he had not planned it, but neither did he resist it. In law the King had the upper hand in the situation, but Henry had other worries on a national scale diverting his attention as he spent a sombre Christmas at Gloucester in the uncomfortable company of Peter des Roches and Peter de Rievaulx. All three were now taking sidelong glances at each other to try and second-guess their best method of both individual and collective survival. It had taken most of the year to quell a Welsh uprising, but the truce was only temporary; Llywelyn still had his own agenda for ousting the English from the south. Worse still for Henry a powerful new Archbishop of Canterbury, Edmund of Abingdon, had been elected to the see and the King's advisors were quick to inform him that the new primate would be opposing any further Poitevin influence in the land, and taking measures to substantially reduce that which already existed. To underline his policy the archbishop turned a blind eye to the continuing raids on Poitevin interests inflicted by Richard Seward and his partisans.

Following the warning from Canterbury, Henry at this time made a strange move, but one which clearly shows how much implicit power Hubert still retained over his thinking. During the February of 1234 he went to see Margaret at Bury St Edmunds, obviously to discuss Hubert's position and to see if any plans had been formulated at Chepstow about which he should know. That the meeting went more in Hubert's favour than the King's is evidenced by Margaret being granted back into her custody eight of Hubert's confiscated manors. A further concession was a safe-conduct for them to visit the nearby holy site at Bromholm when they should wish – not now a likely option![6] While not an olive branch gesture, Henry was seemingly taking out insurance for his old advisor to be reconsidered under terms yet to be agreed, as the existing Poitevin faction under Peter des Roches and Peter des Rivaulx looked more and more like becoming a spent force. That moment arrived with considerable speed, immediately after Edmund of Abingdon's consecration on 2 April 1234. Barely a week later, at a Westminster council, the dynamic archbishop demanded the King remove the two premier Poitevins from power, their roles to be absorbed under Edmund's archiepiscopacy as hereditary chief English advisor to the crown. By the end of April this had been enacted and the detested Poitevins ousted. Peter des Roches and his yes-man Peter de Rivallis went and found anonymity in Winchester Cathedral; Stephen de Segrave took off to St Mary's Leicester, while Robert Passelewe was later found in the depths of the Temple in the city of London.

The celebrations within the walls of Chester can be imagined! This done, the archbishop set about restoring law and order to a populace aggrieved by the illegal confiscation of their lands by the Poitevin faction. Hubert, as always well informed of events concerning his well-being, knew it would not be long before Edmund's messenger would be knocking at Chepstow Castle door. The call came in May (via Hubert's new intermediary, the Dominican prior of Bristol) with a summons for Hubert and the other rebels to attend the King and court at Gloucester. There, on the 28th of the month, under Edmund's safe conduct, Hubert and Henry came once more face to face. Hubert's old friend, Matthew Paris, was there too,

There came to the peace of the king, by the mediation of the archbishop and the bishops, Hubert de Burgh, once justiciar of England, whom the king, regarding him with a calm look, took into his embrace and gave him the kiss of peace, restoring to him his former favour, along with the other exiles.[7]

Chapter 15

1234–1243 The Sunset Years of England's Elder Statesman

Hubert's restoration to court life was under way. But he above all others knew that his previous high standing with the King would neither be automatic, nor happen overnight, and most likely not even exist at all in its former extent. Many changes of fortune during the last two years, both Henry's and Hubert's, were irreversible, much common ground on new terms would have to be established before both could regard each other with equanimity again. Hubert, now in his seventies, was well aware that Henry, just 27, retained his inherent Angevin capability to reverse his thinking and renege on former agreements with any of his court – think Bromholm! Where Henry's vulnerability might be perceived would be in his relationship with Edmund of Canterbury, so Hubert, as before, sought to find episcopal safeguards along the way on his return to high office.

Almost immediately Hubert received the news that both he and the others who had assisted in his survival were no longer considered legally as outlaws, their normal citizenry status was restored with immediate effect by the King's court, this being chaired by probably the most fair and clear-minded jurist of his day, Judge William de Raleigh. The original decision to make them outside the law and so capable of being apprehended by anyone had been Henry's, but the law of the land required that only a court of law could deliver a verdict of outlawry, consequently Hubert was able to kick-start his rehabilitation with a recovery of his possessions which had been forfeited during the period of his illegally imposed outlawry. And the same judgement applied to the rebels who had sided with and saved Hubert, namely Richard Seward and his followers. Also, because Irish rebels had murdered the young Richard Marshal, Earl of Pembroke, in Ireland during their orgy of savage recrimination against any opposition, Henry now bestowed a knighthood and the great and ancient earldom of Pembroke upon his brother, Gilbert Marshal. (Tragically, young Gilbert was to die in a tournament in 1241.)

The reversal of Henry's illegal outlawry allowed Hubert to start the legal process to take back his Three Castles in Wales and his favourite East Anglian lands headed by Hadleigh Castle. Other important castles and properties he now recovered were in Lincolnshire, Bedfordshire, Nottinghamshire, Suffolk, Dorset and Staffordshire. He had retained his earldom of Kent throughout his persecution and now, month by month, was able to see his income from his reacquired lands start to accumulate. Likewise, his substantial personal treasure which had been ordered into the safe custody of the Knights Templar vaults in the City of London, Hubert was now able to legally recover.[1] By July 1234 he had regained sufficient respect to once more attend the King's Westminster councils. He was no longer Justiciar, that post had been granted to Stephen de Segrave, but now he, along with the other Poitevin court clique, were out of favour (and out of town) Henry had decided that the post of Justiciar, which came with the Conqueror in 1066, should now lapse. The new archbishop, Edmund of Canterbury, was the King's principal advisor in all matters so, probably on Edmund's advice, Henry took the decision that both he personally, and his administration politically, had outgrown the need for a Justiciar as national mentor. Hubert minded not a jot, he had given his best years to that office and now, with the Poitevins finally ousted, the relative stability of the kingdom as run by a now newly formed and largely English government owed much of that stability to Hubert's measures imposed in his earlier times as Justiciar, when he retained a corporate English governmental voice, often against the bitterest opposition. The lacklustre King now found himself being advised by the all-powerful Edmund instead of Hubert; the old courtier however, could not but help keeping an albeit somewhat arthritic finger on the pulse of events, consequently he appears in regular attendance on sittings of the royal council during the years 1234–1236. Ever influential – not what you know, but who – Hubert was again a background driving force in re-establishing a relatively stable Irish government. His nephew, Richard de Burgh, against concerted opposition, was restored in October 1234 to the ownership of Connaught in Ireland; the following year Richard was to finally subdue the militant O'Connor faction. All this time Hubert was overseeing his team of lawyers who were making small fortunes for themselves in pursuing the documentary reclamation processes to legally reinstate most of his former lands and honours. Consequently, in December 1235, he was at last able to legally recover the ownership of his highly prized Three Castles of the Justiciar in the south Wales marches. Soon he was able to tot up that he had recovered the ownership of five of his old castles, along with most of their subsidiary estates. These stacked up to a comfortable pension with which to ease into his last years.

During what was to be the last decade of his life Hubert divided his time between semi-retirement at his Surrey country estate at Banstead and enjoying social gatherings at his Westminster mansion. With him at all times was of course Margaret, with Megotta and John never far away and popping in to see their father. Though he did not now have any defined role at Court, Hubert's voice was still too influential to ignore, and he looked to keep his mind sharp with the now fast-moving political scenario of these 'new dawn' days at Court. He was accorded his own special place when called to attend councils at Westminster; also Henry still required that his Earl of Kent, when requested, add his name as witness to many important state documents. There were still great ceremonial occasions too where, garbed in the heraldic vestments of his earldom, Hubert could take his place as a senior peer of the realm; several such events came at once in January 1236. The first was on the 14th when the whole Court travelled down to Canterbury Cathedral for the wedding of Henry to the 14-year-old Eleanor of Provence, daughter of Raymond Berenguer, Count of Provence, and Beatrice of Savoy. Archbishop of Canterbury (and old Mertonian) Edmund Rich conducted the ceremony. It must have been one which Margaret and Megotta especially enjoyed seeing, with Eleanor – all accounts describe her as exceptionally beautiful – in her shimmering, pleated golden gown. Eleanor also brought with her the golden rose of Provence which was to become the badge of the English monarchs thereafter. Although some were to change the colour from Provençal gold to Lancastrian red, then to Yorkist white, the royal arms continue today to display the united white and red rose 'slipped and leaved proper'. But Eleanor was from the great and ancient Savoy family, the influence of which extended across most of Europe. So with the marriage came another resurgence of continental influence on the irresolute Henry, combined with an influx of rapacious foreigners from the continent – this time the Savoyards – which must have been an anathema for Hubert. He was not to live to see it but his outrage could be imagined at the gift in 1263 of Henry to the Savoyards of land by the Thames in the Strand on which to build their Palace of Savoy. But his spirit looking down in later years would probably have been better pleased when Eleanor was attacked by native Londoners, who hated her, and pelted her in the street with stones, offal, and rotten vegetation.

On 23 January Hubert went to Merton Priory for a conference the outcome of which was to extract the beginnings of English parliamentary law from the chapters of Magna Charta. In the previous November Henry had adjourned a legal hearing in London and ordered it to be heard instead by a *parliamentum* – a meeting of the Great Council of peers. The meeting was moved from the legal chambers at Westminster to Merton Priory because the Westminster law courts were flooded and the Priory offered the best equivalent conference facilities space near to London. The meeting of the Great Council decided that the King should defer to the Common Council decisions of the peers as the rules of Magna Charta dictated, and not to the views of '"foreigners" in the country'. Henry acceded to their argument and on Wednesday 23 January, the formal 'Statute of Merton' was placed on the nation's statute books as The Commons Act 1236 (20 Hen 3 c.4). The rights enshrined in this 11-chapter statute would next be revised in 1948. Hubert would have taken great interest in these proceedings, having followed the life of Magna Charta from its inception perhaps more closely and personally than any others in the court. He would have also found his first face-to-face meeting at the conference with the social tsunami that was the young 28-year-old Simon de Montfort, an enlightening occasion. Arriving in England from his native Normandy in 1230 de Montfort (Henry III's brother-in-law), now based in Kenilworth, recovered the earldom of Leicester lost by the sixth earl. He would later, in 1258 at Oxford, succeed in building on the base that Hubert had helped create, by setting in place the first recognizable English Parliament of Commoners, or in Sir Winston Churchill's words 'a durable legislative assembly'. When the conference broke up, as a parting gift to the Priory for successfully hosting the event, Henry gave to Prior Henry de Basinges a tun of best Gascony wine – 900l it will be remembered!

Hubert then had to hotfoot it to his last January outing – the coronation in Westminster Abbey of Eleanor as Queen of England on Sunday 20 January. It was conducted with all the pomp and pageantry that Henry could arrange, starting with a long procession of European royalty, peers and barons, headed by the state trumpeters. In the Abbey Hubert would have looked on with a critical eye as four Cinque Ports barons carried the Canopy for the first recorded time at a Queen's coronation: he would have known them all. He would have been mightily impressed by their dress of scarlet satin doublet with gold buttons, sleeves slashed with purple satin, muslin ruffs, crimson silk hose, white shoes, all topped with a black velvet Spanish hat with one scarlet and two black ostrich feathers. They certainly made an impression! Simon de Montfort made an impression too – on Eleanor, who asked Henry who he was. Henry replied 'An ambitious young man'. Just how ambitious Simon was, Henry would soon learn.

Not long after the marriage of Henry and Eleanor a spin-off occurred concerning the new Queen's uncle, William of Savoy, which nearly caught Hubert off guard. Henry apparently had made some kind of agreement to contract to marry into William's family the young Richard de Clare, heir to the vastly rich earldoms of Gloucester and Hertford. As earlier noted, Richard de Clare had been a ward of Hubert's since 1231. However, during the time Hubert was on the run and his potential fate looking likely to be death, Margaret had looked to her own and her children's security by secretly arranging the betrothal of Richard to Megotta. But she didn't inform Henry, and appears not to have fully informed Hubert of this fact subsequent to his eventual survival. Hubert was too astute not to have become aware of the situation as soon as he settled back with his family and most likely agreed with Margaret for them both to keep quiet on the matter until, and if, it came out into open. This it now did, to Henry's considerable displeasure. In his defence, submitted at a hearing with the king at Eagle village in Kesteven, (a meeting place of the Knights Templar), Hubert claimed no knowledge of Margaret's contract made in the summer of 1232, being then *incommunicado* with his family owing to his persecution, but he now asked to be granted time to pursue a legal annulment of the supposed betrothal. His request was granted, being given until Easter 1237. Countess Margaret and Hubert could breathe again. But when that deadline came around Henry was engrossed in other state affairs, mostly involving raising contentious taxes and so further deferred hearing Hubert's case. Oddly, soon afterwards Hubert was required to be present at the meeting of the King's council with the barons who finally acceded to the King's tax provisions. The much postponed de Clare meeting was never to take place, and for the most heartbreaking of reasons. While staying at the family home at Burgh in Norfolk, Megotta succumbed to illness and died there towards the end of October 1237. Perhaps too, who knows, the public humiliation of the secret 'marriage' with all the attendant gossip and witch-hunting, took its toll on the youngster. Her distraught parents conveyed their favourite child's body to the Priory church of the Blackfriars in London for interment with due ceremony, en route resting for a night in the abbey of St Albans. In gratitude of the abbot's benevolence Hubert gave the abbey a silken hanging.[2] Subsequently, on 26 January 1238, the 15-year-old Richard de Clare was married to Maud de Lacy.

Prior to this family tragedy, Hubert's Scots wife Margaret would have had cause to celebrate on 25 September 1237 when the Treaty of York was signed there between King Alexander II of Scotland and Henry III of England. This treaty decisively settled the Anglo-Scots border as running from the Solway Firth in the west to the mouth of the River Tweed in the east. It remains so today.

Hubert was now little concerned in the great national decisions to which he would once have been central as he now started to take even more of a back seat in public life. He had outlived virtually all of his contemporaries; a fact brought home to him with the death of his prime enemy Peter des Roches on 9 June 1238. But his ungrateful monarch was determined to hound him to the last, accusing Hubert again of treachery in past times, purely for the motive of being able to confiscate his lands in punishment and so possess them in forfeit on the old earl's death. Once again in July 1239 his legal clerk, Laurence of St Albans, presented his defence in such a lucid and literate exposition as to outmanoeuvre the jealous Henry, and Hubert verbally rebutted the monarch on the accusation of treason with the resounding rejoinder 'I have never been a traitor to you or to your father, and by God's grace this is now apparent in you!'[3] Matthew Paris, who includes Hubert's defence in his Chronicle,[4] explains this to mean 'If I had wished to betray you, the kingdom would not be yours today.' At the final hearing on the trumped up charges the King again took back the Three Castles in Wales and Hubert's Hadleigh estate. He also decided not to pursue the Richard de Clare matter further. As the sympathetic Paris records, 'The old earl suffered all the king's ingratitude and rudeness, reproach and contumely, even all the reverses of fortune, with equanimity and patience.'[5]

In 1239, as one of his final acts in putting his financial affairs into good order, Hubert passed the patronage of his Maison Dieu hospital at Dover into royal care. He knew Henry well enough to be sure he would not tamper with anything episcopal, and so it proved, for the Maison Dieu continued in its original role of caring for Dover's poor until the ecclesiastical ravages of a later monarch in 1535 (which it survived – just!). About now, in 1240, Hubert also signed the sale deeds transferring the ownership of his London estate from the trust deed of 1230 to the ownership of Archbishop of York, Walter de Gray. Its subsequent story is told below.

By 1241 Hubert had retired completely to quiet solace at his country home: there was no longer any reason for him to be at Court. If, on occasion, his opinion was required by any of Henry's advisors, then the meeting would be at Banstead. Doubtless the up and coming courtiers sent down to him looked forward to a day out in the country enjoying the hospitality of the grand old man. They would return to London having been enthralled by his reminiscences of times long before the youngsters had been born, as when he been a young squire in the Lionheart's court, or loyally fought John's hopeless causes across Normandy. His heroics at Chinon, and the amazing Battle of Sandwich still, a quarter of a century later, spoken of in hushed respectful tones whenever raised as a topic at court, and not least, the epoch days of Magna Charta at Runnymede. In today's terms it might be likened to hearing first-hand accounts of a Hurricane pilot's experiences in the Battle of Britain. Margaret, never leaving his side, doubtless too told the old earl off for boring their guests with his war stories. But in these medieval days warfare was never for long a distant memory, as Hubert was to be painfully and finally reminded. In 1242 Henry set out on yet another abortive military expedition across the continent; with him as military commanders went Hubert's son John and his nephew Richard, son of his elder brother William. Like Hubert's other nephew Reymond, the young Richard was to die in action in France, but Hubert's thanks went heavenward on the safe return of John who, like father like son, acquitted himself with exceptional bravery in the Battle of Saintes.[6] This battle ended Henry's 'last chance' campaign to beat the French on their own soil. He had joined forces with Count Hugh de Lusignan against Louis IX in a revolt fomented by John's widow, Isabella of Angoulême, wife of Count Hugh. As Hubert might have told him, Henry found himself hopelessly outnumbered by the French at Saintes and was forced to sign a five-year non-aggression truce with the French King in January 1243, known as the Peace of Lorris. Hubert could now watch it all with his feet up from his favourite armchair at Banstead in the knowledge that Henry was now for others to worry about.

Throughout his court life Hubert had been generous to religious foundations, especially in Kent and East Anglia where many of his financial legacies lasted for decades after his passing. Principal of these, of course, being the Maison Dieu at Dover, as noted above. In physical gifts too he was munificent, presenting Salisbury Cathedral in 1225 with a book of texts bound in gold and set 'with precious stones and relics of divers saints'. At Rochester Cathedral, he presented and dedicated a window to St William. Neither of these latter has survived, but Rochester claims to display a Victorian copy window of Hubert's supposed original. Perhaps Hubert de Burgh's most interesting and lasting legacy was one on a national scale, and one he could never have foreseen. Living now more or less permanently at Banstead, he had decided to sell his Westminster property some time ago: it stretched along the Thames, a little way behind today's Banqueting House. Avoiding the King's rapacious appetite for other people's property, back in 1230 Hubert had transferred his mansion into a trusteeship, but with the proviso that when it was eventually sold the proceeds were to be put to the relief of the Holy Land.[7] By this means he could absolve himself of the Crusades obligation he had verbally made during his self-preservation rigours of 1232. About the year 1240 the trustees accepted an offer from the Archbishop of York, Walter de Grey, of £400 for the estate. A few years later, in 1245, the archbishop was to sell the property, now called York Place, and described as 'our houses in the street of Westminster, with the rents gardens, vivaries, and all other appurtenances', to the see of York as its permanent palace in London. So it was to remain until 1529 when the then cardinal Archbishop of York, Thomas Wolsey, was ousted from office and the palace confiscated by Henry VIII to be a wedding present to Ann Boleyn. Hubert's old mansion by then had been enhanced by twenty-four Primates of York, including three cardinals, into the most opulent palace in London. But Henry VIII was to make it even more magnificent, he also renamed it, as 'Whitehall'.[8] And so it has been down to today, the nominal seat of English national governmental authority – Hubert would have been well pleased! William Shakespeare later noted the name-change in his play *Henry VIII*:

> Sir, you must no more call it York Place, that's past, for since the cardinal fell that title's lost, 'tis now the king's and call'd Whitehall.

On 12 May 1243, at Banstead, Countess Margaret de Burgh gently closed the fading eyes of her beloved husband. With a dignity appropriate to the greatest statesman of his times, Hubert de Burgh's coffin was reverently borne to London for a ceremonial burial at the Priory of the Blackfriars where he was laid to rest beside his adored Megotta. His lifetime chronicler Matthew Paris summarized his passing with due reverence,

> And in these same days, the Earl of Kent, Hubert de Burgh, full of days, after many arbitrary attacks and persecutions of the king, and after the most varied vicissitudes of fortune, on the twelfth of May in the most laudable manner ended his days at his Manor of Banstead. And his venerable body was carried with reverence to be buried at London in the house of the Friar Preachers to whom in life he had presented many gifts.[9]

Margaret de Burgh was to live on in a lonely widowhood until in 1259 she joined her husband and daughter.

In the Introduction we made a first acquaintance with Matthew Paris: he knew Hubert on a personal basis better than most and told us much of what we know about him today, so a brief valedictory concluding note here about this polymath monk might not be out of place. Paris himself would also live on to 1259 in his St Alban's monastery, writing his historical accounts of his times, embellished with his incomparable illustrations and maps. He served St Alban's Abbey for forty-two years. Perhaps the best source descriptive of his achievements exists in the Oxford Dictionary of National Biography which devotes fourteen closely typed pages to his huge output. Within that opus Hubert de Burgh gets frequent mentions. In his famous *Chronica Majora* Matthew Paris wrote up his end-of-year summary of events for 1243,

> This year, therefore, passed over, threatening danger and trouble to the church, plentiful enough in vegetables and fruits, bringing death and annoyance to many nobles in Christendom, reproachful and prejudicial to the kingdom and king of England, bringing battles and hostilities for the Italians, and mistrust for the Holy Land, and generating schism and scandal between the Templars and Hospitallers.

His somewhat negative views of that year would have been reinforced by Hubert's death – a man he held in the greatest esteem for all the years that they knew each other.

Hubert de Burgh is not recalled in today's history, the foregoing account asks only that perhaps it is time he was. Viewed from the secure distance of some eight centuries his life seems the stuff of modern adventure, filled with intrigues, chases, challenges, battles, and victories. But it has to be remembered that he was living it in his day, for real. Every day that Hubert got out of bed was another day where survival counted above all else and, as this account has hopefully shown, he was a pre-eminent expert in that art, not only in the field of battle but also in the equally lethal arena of international politics. Few, if any, statesmen in the last one thousand years can claim to equal his example of outstanding personal dedication and heroism in the cause of his country.

Chapter 16

In Memoriam

Toxxday, and quite appropriately, perhaps the most tangible memory of Hubert de Burgh survives in the castles with which he was most closely associated – the writer is not aware of any specific statue or other memorial erected to his memory, except of course the Dover Maison Dieu described below.

Principal among these castles must be Dover. Still largely as it was in Hubert's days – its towering solidity atop the White Cliffs offering a perennial and salutary monument in definition of English resistance to uninvited visitors. It has been garrisoned continuously since before Hubert's day up to 1958. Second in importance, Hadleigh in Essex, though now a ruin, continues to impress the visitor with its purposeful massive walls and tower remnants; still implacably keeping watch across the Thames Estuary in protection of London and, as well, Hubert's East Anglian homelands. Later, both Edward II and Edward III often stayed there for a break out of London; also various royal princes held the estate in the fifteenth century including Edward, Duke of York (1400–1415) and Duke Humphrey of Gloucester (1415–1457.) By the time of Lord Rich's ownership in 1552, however, it had become uninhabitable.[1] Hubert's personal 'Three Castles of the Justiciar' in south Wales – Skenfrith, Grosmont and Whitecastle – are today in the skilled care of the Welsh Historic Monuments office. Their isolation, even today, evokes the constant danger of attack by the Welsh that always threatened their incumbents, regardless of the care which Hubert expended on their upkeep and fortifications. Hubert had two other castles built in the north for administration of his county properties there, Knaresborough in Yorkshire, and Hornby in Lancashire. Knaresborough was demolished in 1310, the present building remains date from Edward III's reign, while at Hornby little survives of Hubert's work following extensive additions to the castle in Henry VIII's reign. Back in Dover, the non-military reminder of

Hubert's life there exists in his Maison Dieu in the town centre. Not that much altered in its original aims as a socially beneficent centre, it continues today as, according to the corporation brochure, 'a living building ... used for conferences, banquets, fairs and concerts'. It does display some impressive Victorian pre-Raphaelite stained glass windows depicting a wide range of notable men who have over the centuries been associated with Dover. Hubert de Burgh is centrally depicted amongst these, also Henry II, and Henry III, also William Longsword, to name a few.

Along the coast in Sandwich, and also very much a 'living' building, is to be found the Chapel dedicated to St Bartholomew after Hubert's victory outside in the Channel over the French on 24 August 1217. It stands within an enclosing sixteen almshouses dating from 1190. Every year at the Chapel, on the saint's anniversary date, is held a patronal service at which time prayers are offered to the continuing memory of the original benefactors, townspeople Hubert would have known well. The service is accepted as one of the oldest commemorations regularly held in this country.[2] (In recent times the decision has been taken to include the Chapel in the United Kingdom National Inventory of War Memorials.)

Somewhat further afield, in Hubert's homeland, survives Creake Abbey, about four miles to the south of Burnham Market in Norfolk. Originally a small chapel founded in 1206 by Sir Robert and Lady Alice de Nerford, an uncle and aunt to Hubert, it was substantially enlarged in 1217 as a memorial both to Hubert's victory and to Sir Robert who was a principal fleet commander at the Battle of Sandwich. Hubert saw to it also that Henry III granted it abbatial status by a charter of 26 October 1231. Happily much remains of the original structure.[3]

At Burgh-next-Aylsham the church of St Mary also benefited from Hubert's philanthropy. Still visible today is what Nikolaus Pevsner described as 'the finest Early English chancel in East Anglia'. However, at present-day Banstead one will look in vain for remains of Hubert's country mansion, the nearby locality Burgh Heath offering the only nominal clue. Three centuries ago the antiquary John Aubrey had rather better luck, or so he thought. He found, 'at the East End of the Church-Yard, in a Field, is a deep Pit sunk, said to be the Remains of the Cellars belonging to the Seat of Hugh de Burgo, Counsellor to King Henry III.'

The Victorian historian of Banstead, HCM Lambert, writing around 1900, also tantalizingly records an accidental find made by a flint miner working 'on the south side of Banstead churchyard' of 'a large quantity of tiles, some of which have a blue line between the red outside and inside, some large blocks of stone, a little stained glass some fragments of pottery and a portion of a capital carved in a fleur de lys'.

At the time it was thought a connection could be made between the site and the Priory of St John of Jerusalem, thus the relics were said to have been removed to the Priory's library at Clerkenwell in London, but currently these have yet to be traced there. Nor was Aubrey's claim ever followed up. The manor found a brief new life as an occasional royal residence for a century or so from 1275, being mostly used by queen consorts; though Edward I stayed there in the winter of 1276–7 and Edward III likewise in 1372–3.

Merton Priory has long gone, but miraculously its original main entrance gate survives in the Merton churchyard of St Mary the Virgin; so it is possible to touch the actual stonework touched by Hubert as he came and went there nearly eight centuries ago. The foundation stones of the Priory's historic Chapter House can also be seen nearby, preserved under modern buildings.

The last resting place of Hubert and his family at Blackfriars has also been long gone. The Dominicans officiated at the family interments when the Priory was located at its original site near Shoe Lane, Holborn, on land originally provided by Hubert in 1224, it will be recalled. By 1276 the order had outgrown this site and moved to much more extensive premises bordering the Thames at Ludgate Hill. The remains of Hubert, Margaret and Megotta were translated with due reverence to the new Priory, along with many other notables. By an odd historical coincidence just off Ludgate Hill there was for centuries a place called Seacoal Lane. It took its name from being the Thames wharf where coal shipped in from the north-east for firing lime-kilns was unloaded and stored. This had its origins in John's reign when Newcastle upon Tyne received its 'privilege' from the monarch to operate the Seacoal Lane locality as a business venture. It was confirmed for continued operations in 1234 by Henry III. It must have been cheek-by-jowl with the Blackfriars Priory burial grounds: and was the source of numerous complaints about its offensive smoke clouds. This disturbance plus the ravages of war and new building and rebuilding on the site have totally erased all that once existed at Ludgate Hill. The Guildhall Library half a mile away will direct the interested enquirer to what documentary records remain to tell the story of the Blackfriars. In France can still be seen the massive fortifications of Chinon, continuing to dominate its surroundings: one wonders at the martial skill of the man who kept an entire French army outside its walls for most of two years.

In 1964 in the underground chapel dedicated to Sainte-Radegonde, beneath the Chinon fortress buildings was uncovered a wonderful wall painting dating from Hubert de Burgh's time. In full colour, it depicts a man and a woman with two younger persons riding out to an unknown destination. Experts tentatively agree the adult riders to be Henry II and one of his daughters Eleanor of Aquitaine, accompanied by two of their sons. If Hubert ever saw the painting he for sure would know who they were.

Lastly, further south at Niort, the castle from which Hubert, as Seneschal of Poitou, governed an area as big as Ireland in what is modern France, perpetuates in the solidity of its still daunting towers the memory of its one-time castellan's unswerving and single-minded authority.

Postscript

At Dover today, standing outside the castle and surveying the French coast, is to be seen the statue of Admiral Sir Bertram Ramsay. It was erected there in November 2000 to commemorate his command of Operation Dynamo (the Dunkirk evacuation) in June 1940. Perhaps at some future time a similar statue (sited nearby) of Hubert de Burgh will merit consideration as an equivalent national hero, who also in his turn (and time) looked out across the Channel for the threat of continental war – and, as Ramsay, was successful in his countermeasures.

Appendix

The inventory of Hubert's treasure deposited with the London Templars for safe custody, the contemporary value being based on the bullion weight of the article. (Close Rolls, 7 February, 1233)

2 gold rings, one having a *balas* ruby, the other an emerald (*balas* = coloured pale rose-red, to orange.)

A sapphire and garnet gold brooch.

12 silk girdles.

3 gold circlets, one with sapphires from the King's old treasure, the other two smaller, of Paris work.

A great cup with figures in relief.

28 cups of silver gilt worked in relief, £125 6s 5d.

57 cups of silver gilt, engraved, £183 1s 11d.

64 plain cups of silver gilt, £199 3s 9d.

9 cups of white silver, £23 14s 6d.

9 silver justs, 8 gilt and 1 white, £55 9s 3d.

22 pairs of basons, £81 1s 9d.

7 porringers, 3 silver salt cellars, £18 19s.

1 crystal phial fitted with silver gilt.

2 silver candelabras £5 9s 6d.

In pennies, £150.

Treasure of Margaret, his wife.

A silver cross, double gilt with a ruby and emerald, relics and figures of St Mary and St John.

A silver porringer with a font, £1 7s 3d.

A gryphon's egg cup £1.

2 white cups, £4 10s.

2 other cups of unknown weight.

2 silver gilt cups, plain £4 6s.

Notes and References

Chapter 1

1. Genealogists have long argued over Hubert's exact ancestry; see, for instance, Planche and Johnston.
2. Smith, LM, (ed.) *The Making of Britain: the Middle Ages* (Macmillan, 1985) p. 34.
3. Carpenter DA, *The Struggle for Mastery: Britain 1066–1284* (Penguin, Allen Lane, 2003) p. 197.
4. The Dialogue, or *Dialogus de Scaccario*, survives as the earliest official manual describing the work of a government department. Tongue in cheek, it could be called 'HMSO Publication No.1'.
5. And these East Anglian '*inquisitiones*' have been saved to this day: the only Domesday questionnaires to survive. They are to be seen in the British Library as *Inquisitio Eliensis* (the Ely Inquest).
6. Today, some eight centuries on, obviously no specific written itinerary survives to tell us exactly how Hubert arrived at the royal court to commence his career. Nevertheless, the foregoing résumé is based on places and Court departments that did then exist, that he is known to have worked in or with, and events contemporary to him.

Chapter 2

1. During July–September 1908 TE Lawrence ('of Arabia') cycled some 2,000 miles across France to research his degree thesis *Crusader Castles*. He visited all the surviving structures of those built, defended and lost by the Angevin monarchs. His thesis achieved a First in Modern History at Oxford in 1910.
2. The term 'Crusade' derives from the Latin *crucesignatus* – 'signed with the cross'. Carpenter, *The Struggle* ... p. 455.

Chapter 3

1. Knight, JK, *The Three Castles* (CADW: Welsh Historic Monuments (2000)).

Chapter 4

1. Dugdale, W, (ed.) *Monasticon anglicanum* 6 vols. 6, 1069 (London, 1846).
2. VCH (Kent) I *Victoria County History of Kent* p. 217.
3. Hardy, TD, (ed.) *Rotuli litterrarum patentum in turri Londinensi asservati* (Rot.Pat.) 11 Aug 1202, 2vols. (London, 1835) p. 16.
4. Luard, HR, (ed.) *Annals of Margam* in *Annales Monastici* (Rolls Series 1 1864); *Roger of Wendover, Flores Historiarum* (Rolls Series 95 1890).

5. It was common practice amongst these archers to stand arrows and crossbow bolts point down in excrement for some time before use so that just a flesh wound inflicted by them would putrefy and poison the injured beyond the medical help of the day. In 1139 the 2nd Lateran Council had tried to ban crossbows as a weapon of military belligerence, except against 'infidels'.

Chapter 5
1. Guilmant, A, *Bygone Rye and Winchelsea* (Phillimore, 1984). *passim*
2. Brooks FW, *The English Naval Forces 1197–1272* (London, 1962) p. 85.
3. Wendover, I.
4. Pipe Roll 7 John, p. 10 & 14 John p. xix.
5. Historians have never agreed upon Hubert's exact marriage details, see Planche for instance.
6. Hajdu, R, 'Castles, castellans and the structure of politics in Poitou 1152–1271' *Journal of Medieval History* IV (1978) p. 30. *passim*

Chapter 6
1. Taylor, CH, (ed.) *The anti-foreign movement in England, 1231–1232* Anniversary Essays in Medieval History by students of Charles Homer Haskins (New York, 1929). *passim*
2. Duby, G, *The Legend of Bouvines* (Polity Press, 1990) p. 26.
3. Duby, pp. 37–54.

Chapter 7
1. Carpenter, *The Struggle* … p. 198.
2. Rothwell, H, (ed.) *English Historical Documents* Vol. III 1189–1327 (Eyre & Spottiswode, 1975) p. 320. *et seq.*
3. Cotton MSS, Augustus ii. 106 and Cotton MSS Charter XIII 31a.
4. *Archaelogia Cantiana*, Vol. I 1858, pp. 52–55.
5. Turner, RV, pp. 64–65.
6. Paris, Matthew, *Chronica majora* (ed.) HR Luard 7 vols. VI, 65 (London, 1872–1883).

Chapter 8
1. Rothwell, p. 324.
2. Paris, Matthew *Chronica Majora*, III, 28.
3. Adams, M, *Smallhythe Place* (National Trust, 2000).
4. Stephens, GR, *A note on William of Cassingham* (Speculum xvi, 1941) p. 220, n. 10, p. 222.
5. *Norman and Saxon*, Rudyard Kipling.

Chapter 9
1. Cannon, HL, *Battle of Sandwich and Eustace the Monk* (English Historical Review XXVII, 1912) p. 658.
2. Cannon, p. 659.

3. Rothwell, p. 93.
4. Cannon, pp. 669–670.
5. Rothwell, p. 91.
6. Rodger, NAM, *The Safeguard of the Sea* (Harper Collins, 1997) p. 55.
7. Stephens, p. 222.

Chapter 10

1. Lambert, HCM, *History of Banstead* (OUP, 1912) p. 217.
2. Knight, JK, *The Three Castles*.
3. West, F, *The Justiciarship in England, 1066–1232* (Cambridge, 1966) p. 248.
4. DNB, *Dictionary of National Biography*.
5. Ellis, C, *Hubert de Burgh: a Study in Constancy* (Phoenix, 1952) p. 177.

Chapter 11

1. Rothwell, p. 5.
2. Ramsay, JH, *A History of the Revenues of the Kings of England 1066–1399* 2vols. I (Oxford, 1925) pp. 274–5.
3. Hardy, TD, I, 495. 526.
4. Brooks, FW, p. 147.
5. Friel, I, *The Good Ship: Ships, Shipbuilding and Technology in England 1200–1520* (London, 1995) p. 68.
6. Friel, p. 69.
7. Planche, JR, 'Genealogical and Heraldic Notices of the Earls of Kent' Vol IX (1854) *Journal of the British Archaeological Association* '... a deed of gift of his house in Southwark to one Alan de Wicton ...' p. 371.
8. Westminster Abbey Cal. f. 347.
9. PRO C 52/34/3.
10. PRO Cart.Ant.Rot.KK34.
11. Martin, W & Toy, S, *The Black Friars in London: a Chapter in National History* (London & Middx. Arch. Soc. Trans., 2nd Series, Vol.5 (1923–29) p. 355.
12. Rodger, p. 59.
13. Wendover II, 33.
14. Hubert's 'Fifteenth' was to prove such a durable governmental financial instrument that it continued on the statute books for another four centuries, until its repeal in 1623.

Chapter 12

1. VCH Kent I, p. 217.
2. Arch.Cant. CXXXVII.
3. Ramsay, I, 274–5.
4. Wendover, II, 379.

Chapter 13

1. Patent Rolls, II, 344–377.
2. VCH Kent I, p. 217.

3. Johnston, SHF, 'The Lands of Hubert de Burgh' *English Historical Review* (1935). *passim*
4. Patent Rolls, II, 422.

Chapter 14
1. Lord, E, *The Knights Templar in Britain* (Pearson, 2004) p. 214. *passim*
2. Taylor, CH. *passim*
3. Sir Maurice Powicke, 'The Oath of Bromholm', *English Historical Review* CCXXIV (October, 1941) p. 541.
4. Wendover, II, 41–42.
5. Carpenter, *The Struggle* ... p. 453.
6. Powicke, 'Bromholm' p. 540 n.1.
7. Paris, III, 290–291.

Chapter 15
1. See Appendix.
2. Powicke, 'Bromholm' p. 105.
3. DNB p. 321.
4. Paris, *Additamenta*.
5. DNB, p. 321.
6. Paris, IV. p. 199.
7. L.C.C.Survey of London, XIII, pp. 4–5.
8. Dugdale, GS, *Whitehall through the Centuries* (Phoenix, 1950) p. 5.
9. Paris, IV, 243–244.

Chapter 16
1. See Powicke, 'Bromholm' p. 546, n.2 for further Hadleigh detail.
2. Burgess, GS, *Two Medieval Outlaws* (Boydell, 1997) p. 6, n. 5.
3. Norfolk Record Society Vol. XXXV.

Select Bibliography

AC, *The Surrenden Charters* (Archaelogia Cantiana Vol. I, 1858).

Adams, M, *Smallhythe Place* (National Trust, 2000).

Altschul, M, *A Baronial Family in Medieval England: The Clares, 1217–1314* (Baltimore, 1965).

Aurell, M, (trans. D. Crouch) *The Plantagenet Empire 1154–1224* (Pearson Education Ltd., 2007).

Baldwin, JW, *The Government of Philip Augustus: Foundations of French Royal Power in the Middle Ages* (Berkeley, 1986).

Barber, R, *The Devil's Crown* (BBC Publns., 1978).

Barker, B, *The Symbols of Sovereignty* (David & Charles, 1979).

Bates, D & Curry, A, (eds.) *England and Normandy in the Middle Ages* (Hambledon, 1994).

Blaxland, G, *South East England: Eternal Battleground* (1981).

Bolton, JL, *The Medieval English Economy 1150–1500* (Manchester UP, 1980).

Boyd, D, *Eleanor, April Queen of Aquitaine* (Stroud, 2004).

Bradbury, J, *Philip Augustus, King of France 1180–1223* (Addison Wesley Publ., 1998).

Britnell, R & Campbell, B, (eds.) *A Commercialising Economy. England 1086–1300* (Manchester, 1995).

Brooks, FW, *The English Naval Forces 1197–1272* (London, 1962).

Brown, M & Cave, J, *A Touch of Genius: the life of T.E.Lawrence* (JM Dent, 1988).

Brown, RA & Colvin, H, '*Dover Castle*', *The History of the King's Works: The Middle Ages*, Vol. 1) (London, 1963) pp. 629–641.

Burgess, GS, *Two Medieval Outlaws* (Boydell, 1997).

Cannon, HL, *Battle of Sandwich and Eustace the Monk* (English Historical Review XXVII, 1912).

Carpenter, DA, 'The Fall of Hubert de Burgh', *Journal of British Studies* XIX (1980).

Carpenter, DA, *The Struggle for Mastery: Britain 1066–1284* (Penguin, Allen Lane, 2003).

Cazel, FA, *Hubert de Burgh – a dissertation* (unpubl.), (Baltimore, 1948).

Church, SD, *King John: New Interpretations* (Woodbridge, 1999).

Churchill, Sir Winston, *The Island Race* (Cassell, 1964).

Cox, MH, & Norman, P, (eds.) *L.C.C.Survey of London* (Batsford, 1930).

Creasy, ES, *The Invasions of England* (London, 1852).

Cross, PR, *Lordship, Knighthood and Locality: A Study in English Society c.1180–c.1280* (Cambridge, 1991).

Crouch, D, *William Marshal: Court, Career and Chivalry in the Norman Empire 1147–1219* (Longman, 1990).

DNB, *Dictionary of National Biography*.

Duby, G, *The Legend of Bouvines* (Polity Press, 1990).

Dugdale, GS, *Whitehall through the Centuries* (Phoenix, 1950).

Dugdale, W, (ed.) *Monasticon anglicanum* 6 vols. (London, 1846).

Duggan, A, *Devil's Brood: The Angevin Family* (London, 1957).

Dyer, C, *Making a Living in the Middle Ages: The People of Britain 850–1250* (Yale, 2002).

Eggert, H, *The Channel Islands* (Robert Hale, 1980).

Ellis, C, *Hubert de Burgh: a Study in Constancy* (Phoenix, 1952).

Everitt, A, *Continuity and Colonisation: the Evolution of Kentish Settlement* (Leicester, 1986).

Fawcett, FB, *Court Ceremonial* (Gale & Polden, 1937).

Flanagan, MT, *Irish Society, Anglo-Norman Settlers, Angevin Kingship: Interactions in Ireland in the late Twelfth Century* (Oxford, 1989).

Friel, I, *The Good Ship: Ships, Shipbuilding and Technology in England 1200–1520* (London, 1995).

Gater, GH, & Godfrey, WH, *Survey of London*, Vol. XVI, Parish of St Martin-in-the-Fields (L.C.C., 1935).

Gibbs M & Lang J, *Bishops and Reform 1215–1272* (OUP, 1934).

Giles, JA, (trans.) *Roger of Wendover's Flowers of History*, 2 vols. 1849–50 (Repr. Llanerch, 1993, 1996).

Gillingham, J, *Richard I* (Yale U.P., 1999).

Gillingham, J, *The Angevin Empire* (Yale, 1984).

Gillingham, J, *Richard I, Galley-Warfare and Portsmouth: the Beginnings of a Royal Navy, in Thirteenth Century England* VI, ed. M Prestwich, RH Britnell and R Frame (Woodbridge, 1997).

Guilmant, A, *Bygone Rye and Winchelsea* (Phillimore, 1984).

Hajdu, R, 'Castles, castellans and the structure of politics in Poitou 1152–1271' *Journal of Medieval History* IV (1978).

Hallam, E, (ed.) *The Plantagenet Encyclopaedia* (Weidenfeld & Nicolson, 1990).

Hardy, TD (ed.) *Rotuli litterrarum patentum in turri Londinensi asservati* (Rot.Pat.) 2vols. (London, 1835).

Harvey, J, *Medieval Craftsmen* (Batsford, 1975).

Haslam, J, *Anglo-Saxon Towns in Southern England* (Chichester, 1984).

Harvey, J, *Medieval Craftsmen* (Batsford, 1975).

Harwood, B, *Hubert de Burgh: Hero of Medieval Dover*, Bygone Kent, Vols.25/8, 25/9, (Meresborough, 2004).

Hearsey, JEN, *Bridge, Church and Palace* (John Murray, 1961).

Hilton, RH, *Peasants, Knights and Heretics* (Cambridge, 1976).

Holden, BW, 'King John, the Braoses, and the Celtic fringe 1207–16' Albion. *Journal of British Studies* Vol. 33:1 (2001).

Holt, JC, *Magna Carta* (Oxford, 1992).

Hozier, HM, *The Invasions of England* 2 vols. (Macmillan, 1876).

Jessup, R & F, *The Cinque Ports* (Batsford, 1952).

Johnston, SHF, 'The Lands of Hubert de Burgh' *English Historical Review* (1935).

Kelly, A, *Eleanor of Aquitaine and the Four Kings* (1950).

Kipling, R, *The Definitive Edition of Rudyard Kipling's Verse* (Hodder & Stoughton, 1946).

Knight, JK, *The Three Castles* (CADW: Welsh Historic Monuments (2000).

Knocker, E, *On the Municipal Records of Dover* (Archaeologia Cantiana, CXXXIV).

Lambert, HCM, *History of Banstead* (OUP, 1912).

Latham, R, & Matthews, W, *The Diary of Samuel Pepys* (Harper Collins, 2000).

Lawrence, TE, *Crusader Castles* (Golden Cockerel Press, London, 1936; Repr. Michael Haag, London, 1986).

Lawrence, TE, *Seven Pillars of Wisdom* (Jonathan Cape, 1940).

Le Patourel, JH, *The Medieval Administration of the Channel Islands 1199–1399* (OUP, 1937).

Lees, BA, *Records of the Templars in England in the Twelfth Century* (Speculum Vol.11 Issue 03 (1935).

Lord, E, *The Knights Templar in Britain*, (Pearson, 2004).

Luard, HR, (ed.) *Annals of Margam* in *Annales Monastici* (Rolls Series 1 1864); *Roger of Wendover, Flores Historiarum* (Rolls Series 95 1890).

MacKenzie, H, *The Anti-Foreign Movement in England, 1231–1232* (Anniversary Essays in Medieval History by Students of Charles Homer Haskins (Boston, 1929).

Martin, W & Toy, S, *The Black Friars in London: a Chapter in National History* (London & Middx. Arch. Soc. Trans., 2nd Series, Vol.5 (1923–29).

Matarasso, F, *The English Castle* (Cassel, 1993).

McLynn, F, *Lionheart & Lackland* (Vintage Books, 2007).

Meyer, P, (ed.) *Histoire de Guillaume le Marechal* (Paris, 1891–1901).

Michel, F, (ed.) *Histoire des Ducs de Normandie et des Rois d'Angleterre* (Paris, 1840).

Mitchell, R & Vann, JM, *Sussex: a Kipling Anthology* (Padda Books, 1990).

Mortimer, R, *Angevin England 1154–1258* (Oxford, 1994).

Murray, KME, *The Constitutional History of the Cinque Ports* (Manchester, 1935).

Norfolk Record Society, *Creake Abbey* (Norfolk Record Society Transactions Vol. XXXV).

Norgate, K, *The Minority of Henry III* (London, 1912).

Norgate, K, *Richard the Lionheart* (London, 1924).

Norgate, K, *John Lackland* (London, 1902).

Oakeshott, RE, *A Knight and his Armour* (Lutterworth Press, 1961).

Oakeshott, RE, *A Knight and his Horse* (Lutterworth Press, 1962).

Oakeshott, RE, *A Knight and his Weapons* (Lutterworth Press, 1964).

Painter, S, *William Marshal: Knight Errant, Baron and Regent of England* (Baltimore, 1933).

Palmer, A & V, *Royal England* (Methuen, 1983).

Paris, Matthew, *Chronica majora* (ed.) HR Luard 7 vols. (London, 1872–1883).

Planche, JR, 'Genealogical and Heraldic Notices of the Earls of Kent' Vol IX (1854) pp. 361–375 *Journal of the British Archaeological Association*.

Poole, AL *From Domesday Book to Magna Carta* (Oxford, 1955).

Powicke, Sir Maurice, *The Thirteenth Century 1216–1307* (OUP, 1962).

Powicke, Sir Maurice, *The Loss of Normandy 1189–1204* (Manchester, 1961).

Powicke, Sir Maurice, 'The Oath of Bromholm', *English Historical Review* CCXXIV (October, 1941).

Prestwich, M, *Armies and Warfare in the Middle Ages* (New Haven and London, 1996).

Ramsay, JH, *A History of the Revenues of the Kings of England 1066–1399* 2vols. (Oxford, 1925).

Richardson, HG, *William of Ely, the King's Treasurer (1195–1215)* (Trans. Royal Hist Soc. XV)

Richardson, HG, *The English Coronation Oath* (Offprint, 1949).

Richardson, HJ, *The English Jewry under Angevin Kings* (Metheun, 1960).

Riley-Smith, J, (ed.) *Oxford Illustrated History of the Crusades* (OUP, 1997).

Rodger, NAM, *The Safeguard of the Sea* (Harper Collins, 1997).

Rosser, G, *Medieval Westminster 1200–1540* (OUP, 1989).

Rothwell, H, (ed.) *English Historical Documents* Vol. III 1189–1327 (Eyre & Spottiswode, 1975).

Round, JH, (ed.) *Ancient Charters prior to 1200 AD* (London, 1888).

Rye, WB, *Hubert de Burgh, the Justiciary* (Norfolk Antiq. Miscell. 1908).

Schramm, PE, *A History of the English Coronation* (trans. LG Wickham Legg) (Oxford, 1937).

Scott-Giles, CW, (rev.) *Boutell's Heraldry* (Frederick Warne, 1966).

Sitwell, S, *British Architects and Craftsmen* (Pan Books, 1960).

Smith, LM, (ed.) *The Making of Britain: the Middle Ages* (Macmillan, 1985).

Statham, SHR, *The history of the castle, town, and port of Dover* (London, 1899).

Stenton, DM, et al. (eds.) *The Great Rolls of Pipe, 1–17 John* 17 vols. (London, 1933–1964).

Stenton, DM, *English Justice between the Norman Conquest and the Great Charter 1066–1215* (George Allen & Unwin, 1965).

Stephens, G,R, *A note on William of Cassingham* (Speculum xvi, 1941).

Stevenson, J, (ed.) *Radulphi de Coggeshall, Chronicon Anglicanum* (Rolls Series 46) (1875).

Strickland, M, (ed.) *Anglo-Norman Warfare* (Woodbridge, 1992).

Taylor, CH, (ed.) *The anti-foreign movement in England, 1231–1232* Anniversary Essays in Medieval History by students of Charles Homer Haskins (New York, 1929).

Tillyard, EMW, *Shakespeare's History Plays* (Chatto & Windus, 1944).

Turner, RV, *Magna Carta* (Pearson, 2003).

Turner, RV, 'Eleanor of Aquitaine and her children: an inquiry into medieval family attachment', *Journal of Medieval History* Vol. 14, Issue 4 (Dec, 1988) pp. 321–335).

Tyerman, C, *England and the Crusades 1095–1588* (Chicago, 1988).

VCH (Kent), *Victoria County History of Kent*.

Vincent, N, *Peter des Roches Bishop of Winchester 1205–38: An Alien in English Politics* (Cambridge, 2002).

Walker, RF, 'Hubert de Burgh and Wales, 1218–1232', *English Historical Review* CCCXLIV (July, 1972).

Warren, WL, *King John* (Metheun, 1961).

Weiss, M, *The Castellan: the early career of Hubert de Burgh* Viator, Vol. 5 (1974).

West, F, *The Justiciarship in England, 1066–1232* (Cambridge, 1966).

Wormald, F, 'The Rood of Bromholm', *Journal of the Warburg Institute* i, (July, 1937).

Index